THE

Shwetabh Gangwar is a novelist, public speaker, professional problem-solver, and has over two million followers on YouTube. He dedicatedly solves people's problems sent to him on his Instagram, and makes videos on as many as he can. He defines it as the purpose of his life and what truly brings him meaning.

THE
RUDEST
BOOK EVER

**INSANELY PRACTICAL IDEAS TO
FREE YOUR MIND FROM ALL BULLSH*T**

SHWETABH GANGWAR

First published by Westland Publications Private Limited in 2019

1st Floor, A Block, East Wing, Plot No. 40, SP Infocity, Dr MGR Salai, Perungudi, Kandanchavadi, Chennai 600096

Westland and the Westland logo are the trademarks of Westland Publications Private Limited, or its affiliates.

ISBN: 9789388754439

10 9 8 7 6 5 4 3 2

Typeset by SÜRYA, New Delhi

Printed at Thomson Press (India) Ltd

MIX
Paper
FSC FSC® C010615

I dedicate this book to the two people I admire the most in my life—my mom and my wifey. I thank my mom for her indomitable strength that protected the child I was. That protection allowed me to shape the individual in me. I thank my wife for her strong determination and values in life, which influence that individual to become better.

CONTENTS

A SMALL YET IMPORTANT
INTRODUCTION

- This book is a collection of perspectives. It's not about one fucking thing.

- This book does not mean to teach. It is written to make you think, which is why the charged language, the book title, and the harsh approach. Although the book does preach a whole lot, all I want from you is to think about it.

- Essentially, this book is about freeing your mind from all the bullshit you have unknowingly attached yourself to and are suffering from—ranging from ideas of happiness to people in your life. It will rip into everything.

- Because this book is about freeing you, it talks about a lot of things from your life.

- Whenever you disagree with something, write down in detail why, what is your reasoning behind it, and pray to God while reading your reasoning that it doesn't sound like, I disagree because my feelings don't like it.

CHAPTER ONE

YOU ARE A PRODUCT

Hey, buddy, how are you doing? Aren't you glad that you bought this book! Well, we are going to go on a journey together. And as long as you are reading this book, I will be your friend. The only case in which this doesn't apply is if you illegally downloaded this book, in which case, fuck you.

This book is about insanely practical ideas to free you from all bullshit. Let me start by saying this: a lot of this was supposed to be your parents' job. I am not gonna say anything bad about your parents. All I am saying is: if people were products, then what we see around us are really shitty ones. So, clearly, parents are royally fucking up their jobs.

Let me give you an introduction of the world you have been brought into:

The world doesn't give a flying fuck about you. This world is a place full of people that will come in the form of friends, lovers and well-wishers; in the form of emotional adhesives, neatly packaged dreams and aspirational lollipops; in the form of saviours, fixers and salespersons. We are gonna talk about them all.

Anyway, when the time comes, a lot of them will take complete advantage of you, rid you of your emotional innocence and turn your world upside down. It will most definitely happen, history tells you that, no matter who you are or what you do—rich, talented, genius, pretty, strong, powerful, polite, kind, or careful.

So, do you feel prepared?

Let's start with you. You are a product. You are a product with hope attached to it. What does that mean? It means that, one day, you are meant to become this awesome, functional unit **capable** of choosing jobs, careers, relationships, environments and economies on your own volition—that's the hope. The better the choices, the better the product you are—that's the simple law on the basis of which the world judges you.

So, here are a few things about you:

- A person is not born ready.
- A person has to be made ready.
- The person is emotional in nature.
- The person does not know how to learn in the beginning; it knows how to absorb, which means it learns whatever it absorbs from its surroundings. I am talking about when you were a kid.

- The person has to learn how to learn.
- The person can think, but does not know *how* to think, which is why it cannot learn how to learn. This may be confusing, but it will become clear later in the book.
- A person's emotional responses to different experiences create **interpretations** of those experiences, which the person assumes to be true. Therefore, emotional responses become one of the earliest teachers of the person.
- 'Emotional responses' is a garbage teacher, because as a kid, the emotional intelligence is underdeveloped.
- Because the person learns by absorption, the parents and surroundings become the other teachers. Instead of teaching the person how to think, parents and surroundings teach what to think—thereby becoming terrible teachers themselves.
- Teaching what to think stops the product from learning how to think and since the person doesn't learn how to think, it grows up to be confused and clueless regarding how to deal with this world.

In conclusion, the product is very likely to be screwed. The product is you.

NOBODY IS BORN AN IDIOT

You may have said this on many occasions in your life: people are fucking idiots.

But nobody is born an idiot—we unknowingly choose to be idiots because we are not taught the methodologies of **how to think**. When devoid of this knowledge, people unconsciously view what they have learned from parents, surroundings and emotional responses as **factual learnings**.

As you grow older and life becomes harder, without the ability of 'how to think', one naturally falls back on what one knows—which strengthens these 'factual' learnings even more, so much so that at a certain age, they can become unchangeable ideas, biases, prejudices and practices that the individual can no longer abandon.

Now, you may be thinking, *what the fuck is he talking about? Factual learnings? How to think? What to think?* Here is an example: imagine growing up in a place where you only interacted with people of one group. Now, also imagine this group of people having a very strict, single-belief system, strict ideologies and strict doctrines on morality, how to live your life, what's decent and what's not. Now, on top of that, also imagine that they have notions which are not so kind about people of other groups, or other belief systems, or even about women. When you teach the children to think exactly like that, it would be called teaching somebody: **what to think**. Makes sense?

If you are growing up with such teachings, those would be called factual learnings, because they may **appear** factual to you, but aren't necessarily so. They are based on fear and ignorance.

So, with time, when they are not corrected by verification, these factual learnings become factual truths to people. Factual truths means they are incontestable to those who believe them, and they most probably will die by them. And once you believe something that strongly, you become its avid defender. Once we become defenders, we become groups. Once we become groups, we disagree with other groups, and fight, and vote, and celebrate, and denigrate on behalf of whichever ideas align most closely to our 'factual' truths.

THE TYPES OF PRODUCTS AROUND YOU

Based on people who are taught how to think and people who are taught what to think, these are the results:

- A person brought up on **what to think** tends to follow ideas, ideologies and ways of living that echo a relationship with familiarity. We do so, because we feel safe with familiarity. Whatever is familiar to you is known to you well. So, you're most comfortable with it.

- A person brought up on **how to think** tends to question, filter and may abandon ideas, ideologies and ways of living that echo a relationship with familiarity. Familiarity, although safe, does not guarantee soundness.

- A person brought up on **what to think** tends to feel threatened by alien ideas, things, or people, which may end up pushing them more towards what they know and are familiar with.

- A person brought up on **how to think,** when confronted by alien ideas or people, takes an interest in understanding and figuring them out. At the same time, they also inspect the first impressions their mind created. They are not threatened, because practising how to think over the years creates curiosity and an investigative attitude. Therefore, any person, thing or idea that is alien becomes food for thought.

- A person brought up on **what to think** inclines towards asking for solutions for their problems, instead of thinking and finding out things by themselves. This explains the insatiable need for self-help books, the lack of self-reliance, and the explosion of 'clever' people online, teaching people how to be successful, to be a man, a millionaire, a strong woman, smart, clever, slick, handsome and beautiful all at once.

- The person who knows **how to think** will try to find solutions for their problems by thinking on their own, using methods of reasoning, with consideration to mental harmony and bringing smoothness in the functioning of their life. To expand the scope of their knowledge, however, they will read books, watch videos and consume all available information. They seek knowledge because knowledge contains perspectives. And the cultivation of how to think requires a collection of as many varied perspectives as one can gather.

- Lastly, a person who **wasn't** brought up on 'what to think' still functions just the same as people who were taught what to think. It happens because one can be deprived of parental guidance, but that is only one of the teachers. The other teachers, such as surroundings and their emotional responses, still teach them 'what to think'. Basically, 'how to think' cannot be self-taught during the developmental years of a person. You may cite a few exceptions, but this book isn't about exceptional people, it's about people.

YOUR PARENTS PROBABLY MESSED UP

Why are parents largely producing products that are unprepared to face the challenges of this world?

It is a very important question, also a fantastic one. It is both important and fantastic because it sits on the assumptions that:

- All parents want to be parents in the first place.
- People who become parents are mentally prepared to be parents.
- People who become parents are mentally fit to be parents.

Do you know how many reasons there are for having a child?

One can become a parent because the guy forgot to pull out, or the girl—out of some ancient, primitive urge—commanded the guy to not pull out, or he believed he had pulled out but the result said otherwise. People have babies because they like babies, or because they have recently been feeling a sense of incompleteness, or because they hope it will make their lives purposeful again. People have babies because they have reached the age society has deemed right to have a baby. People have babies because it appears to be a viable strategy to save their marriage, or because one of the partners wants to have a baby, and the other complies. People have babies so the baby can grow up to fulfil the unfulfilled dreams of either of the parents.

There is a great chance that you might have been born from one of those reasons. Ideally speaking, there should be a strategy. You are bringing a fucking life into this world, and that person is gonna grow and contribute in many ways to this world. They are gonna vote, follow ideologies, make people money—which is what a job is— find love, marry, and do a lot of other things, like write shitty poetry in their teens.

If they are not a responsible person, they are gonna be hurting a lot of people. And if they grow up to be a douchebag, you are indirectly responsible for hurting all the people that douche is going to hurt. If they grow up to be a follower of ideologies that talk about dividing people, then the parents too are responsible for creating one more follower.

WHY SO MANY SHITTY PRODUCTS?

The question is: how much forethought goes in the minds of parents before having a baby **about the baby**?

If the prime motivation is: *A baby is a cute little thing that will change our lives*, well, that is not good enough. There is a high possibility that you're gonna be creating another moron on this planet. A kid ain't gonna figure shit out by themselves. If they are not gonna be able to, then somebody will use that and make them their follower. And that somebody will probably not give as much of a shit about the kid as the parents would. Unfortunately, this is what happens in most cases. People learn shitty ideas from surroundings, parents and their own underdeveloped emotional intelligence.

And with this, they enter this world.

Now, there is a thing called responsible motivation, which sounds like: *We are creating a human—are we mentally fit and prepared to create a person for whom we will be solely responsible? If not, shall we now start to upgrade our thoughts, perceptions, perspectives, create multiple storages of knowledge—which in time will cater to the young person's curiosities and impact the overall development of its personality?*

'Responsible motivation' means parents realising that they will have one of the strongest influences while the foundation of the personality of the child is being laid. And, to prepare the child, the parents will have to prepare themselves first. Unfortunately, parents on this planet aren't so big on this one.

SHOULD ALL PARENTS BE GENIUSES THEN?

Fuck no, I am not saying that. I realise parents have shit to do. They have jobs, their relationship, finances to manage, and a house to take care of. I realise that they also have to watch television, talk about politics, buy more stuff, make room for the baby, drink tea, fight and argue, battle ageing, wrinkles, receding hairlines, declining morning erections, buy even more stuff, satisfy their parents, satisfy their bosses, satisfy their respective partners, say goodbye to their dreams, accept existential insignificance, and so on and so forth. Yes, there is a hint of sarcasm above.

In many cases, people don't think they need to learn anything because they assume they already know everything—a very dangerous assumption that comes from a frightening absence of self-awareness. So, they believe they are qualified to teach their kid anything there is to know in this world.

Here's the truth: most parents don't have their shit figured out because nobody taught them how to think when they were growing up. In short, they are not philosophers.

PERFECT PARENTS ONLY EXIST IN MOVIES

Ideally, the perfect parents would be:

- Very wise.
- Aware of the child's emotional struggles as it grows.
- Aware of the nature of lessons to give with every phase in the child's life.
- Equipped with the sensitivity and command over ideas to present them in a way which prevents practical ideas from being misused.
- Careful not to over-instruct, which is a form of controlling, thereby obstructing the natural growth of curiosity, learning and exploration of self.
- Curious about the inclinations of the child.
- Aware of when to let the child get hurt and when to intervene.

This means they are not simply sharing ideas and information, they are doing so while considering the impact, need, urgency, application, mood, temperament and learning curve of the individual.

For this, people would have to be fucking philosophers, which they are not, regardless of whether they have degrees in philosophy or not. Therefore, such perfect parents exist as exceptions and in movies.

THE DUMB GOAL OF SHITTY PARENTING

In reality, what we usually get is the widely practised style of parenting, which is:

- Protect the child from accidentally killing themselves, getting killed or hurting themselves.
- Keep them fed and loved and try to discipline them.
- Educate them, and to get them an education.
- Teach them what's right and wrong by distributing punishment and love—punishment when the child messes up or pisses off the parents, and love when the child is being responsible, or depending on the mood of the parent.
- Aspire that they will one day become capable and take care of themselves.

The last point is the main focus. You should be educated, they say. What the fuck does that actually mean? Getting a degree. Now, a degree is not a bad thing. The motivation behind getting a degree, however, is what's important.

For them the motivation is a job, which has three categories: good job, bad job and great job. They want you to get a great job, therefore the degree should come from the best of institutions. *Goddamn, my kid got selected to the best school, I am so happy, I am an awesome parent.*

So, the objective of education is not for you to become a fine, thinking person, but to become someone who earns very well. They realise that rich people have a better life; you will be treated pretty well by your family members, the society that surrounds you and by members of the opposite sex. So it's not entirely unreasonable for them to want you to become a person of status.

What's utterly stupid about it is that it takes care of the status part only, **not** the person. In the phrase 'a person of status', you need the development of both. Status is a socially engineered identity that tends to replace the individual identity. So, status must not dictate who the person is. The person must dictate what to do with the status in accordance with how they feel about that status.

Take all the high-achieving people who hate their jobs or professions. Despite money, achievements and success, they are miserable doing what they do. It happens because a sense of meaning and satisfaction does not come from status; such things are deeper and more personal than that.

Your parents wanted to prepare you to be one of the best products for this world. In action, what they end up doing is: prepare you technically, academically and skill-wise to be the best product for the race, like a car. The human element is barely accounted for.

The goal of most parents is for their child to become capable of achieving great success. If that goal is achieved, in their minds, they are the best parents. What's fucked up about it is, in case you do achieve success, they **assume** that they have somehow prepared you to deal with the world as well—which is utter bullshit.

Now, if you are one of those people whose parents never forced you to do anything, they didn't push you to achieve success, or anything of that sort, they let you do whatever you wanted—I am not saying parents who push their kids are evil. What I am saying is: it is the responsibility of parents to help you grow both into a capable working person **and** a capable **thinking** one. Did they do that?

PARENTS ARE EXPERTS IN ACTING

Learning of any kind that involves zero investment of your thinking produces only imitation. To create ideas and better yourself, you have to take the information and apply your own mind.

When parenting is not coming from the parents' own mind, their own ideas and their own thinking, it becomes an imitation of whatever they have learned. What that means is, they could be playing a character of what they believe a parent is. The character could be of a strict parent, of a genius person who knows everything, or of a person who is very brave and heroic. It could be anything. But when this happens, it becomes harder for the kid to find their parent approachable and figure them out. There is love, but the relationship is between the kid and a character, not the actual person.

There are several reasons for parents to do this.

One reason could be: playing a role gives them the comfort of hiding all their personal trials and tribulations from you. Just because somebody is older doesn't mean they have figured out life. In most cases, older people are children who have aged. Stop attaching maturity, wisdom, enlightenment to ageing. *He is old, hence he must be wise* is one of the stupidest notions we take for granted.

Another reason is pride. In cases where the parents' sole focus is on the kid becoming capable, the character they play also becomes the one that expects only brilliance and exceptional performances from the kid. In playing this character, the kid becomes a reflection of their ego. The kid's emotional and personal growth is hardly ever addressed. There is love, but it is shown in demands of accomplishments and excellence. In this case, what is missing is the responsibility of helping that kid become the individual they are meant to be.

Another reason why most parents don't care to break out of these stupid, empty shells of characters is, they don't even consider that the kid's personality is getting shaped by things that hurt them, influence them and amaze them. The reason for that is, they don't see them as people yet. They see them as kids who must be doing harmless, innocent kids' stuff. No wonder they are shocked beyond belief when they find out their kid was doing some adult stuff. *You were smoking and drinking? You are having sexual relations already? But you are so young!*

The moment a kid touches the age of thirteen, parents should break out of their stupid characters and start looking at their kid as an inexperienced adult. What it means is, they are now thinking of doing everything that adults do.

In conclusion, parenting is largely coming from imitating whatever people learn from the culture in their surroundings. This basically means that whatever parents do is coming from a degree of cluelessness with regards to what to actually do. No wonder you enter adulthood completely clueless.

The point of having a brain should be to minimise error, not having to deal with it endlessly. But you were never taught the mechanisms which would prepare you to protect yourself and understand the errors that produce bothersome situations, hurt and pain. You are left to deal with all of it by yourself. As a result, you're a grown person now, on your own, having to deal with the world telling you your self-worth and net worth; adjusting your self-esteem as you make sense of rejections from people you desire; filling yourself with insecurities and ideas from comparing yourself to god-knows-what standards; and lastly, triggering negative emotions as a response to failures, heartbreaks and denial of wishes. Yes, you are doing that to yourself, the world is doing that to you, and it does that to everybody.

So, without wasting time, let's concern ourselves with arming you with better means, methods and mechanisms to deflect and deal with shit that has happened to you, is happening to you and will happen to you.

CHAPTER TWO

YOU KNOW YOU WANT TO BE SPECIAL

Let's be clear about something: The idea of being special excites almost all of us—to varying degrees, depending upon the individual. It's perfectly normal. Be honest: you know you have fantasised about standing out in certain situations; played and replayed different scenarios of the same meetings and interactions in your mind with you as the centre of attention and master of the perfect dialogue. You have imagined scenarios in which you are born as somebody blessed with what you believe will make you fulfilled. You have wished that, one day, everybody around you would tell you that you are amazing, and treat you like you are amazing. And you have daydreamed about people you want to impress, please and attract instantly wanting to be your friend and lover after meeting you because you're so impressive. Lastly, who hasn't dreamt about having millions of dollars!

THIS IS HOW YOU BECOME SPECIAL

According to you, 'specialness' is being born special, being told you are special, being treated like you are special, and being rich. Unfortunately, all of that has **nothing** to do with specialness. Let's first define what specialness is. During your childhood, there are chances you may have experienced one of these three things: a) you were told you are special, b) you were told you are not special, or c) there was no mention of you being special or un-special at all.

If you were told by your parents that you are special, kindly rinse your mind of that idea immediately. If you were told you are not special, then, no, your parents aren't geniuses; that, too, is completely wrong. Lastly, if there was no mention of specialness in your household, chances are you are still seeking it.

And since all of us are seeking it in either **assuming** *if I do this, it will make me special,* or **wishing** *if only I had this, I would have been special,* you need to understand that specialness is **earned**.

If you were asked, *what were the moments in which you felt special,* you might think of the time when people laughed at your joke, applauded some effort, or when your post on social media got more likes than usual—that would be much closer to the truth for the generation today. Such moments contain all elements of wanting acceptance and approval from others, not of specialness.

Here's a very simple example of specialness: *I felt it when I achieved that.* 'That', is anything that created a considerable amount of self-belief in you, and made you believe for the first time that you are capable. We all assume we are capable, because nobody would like to believe otherwise. But it remains theoretical until you have achieved something that not only becomes a reference point for yourself in the future—*I was able to achieve this, this is who I am*—but also proves to yourself that you have what it takes to be capable—*I believe I can achieve anything I put my mind to.*

Specialness is the badge of realisation you **earn**. It may seem very simple to you, but this thinking can change the course of your life. Any achievement dictates you have created or mastered something. This means that not only did you gain in terms of knowledge, but you built habits of discipline, hard work, prioritising and focusing—habits that will serve you in almost all aspects of life.

On top of that, achievements create immense self-belief; *I can do it because I have done it before* is an amazing thought to have at the back of your mind, guiding you. Also, achievements are rewarded with more opportunities, and give you status in the eyes of society.

Now, imagine setting this up in the mind of a child, instead of telling them out of bias that they are special, or out of spite that they are not. Not mentioning it at all is equally bad, as it simply avoids addressing a want already growing inside the mind of that person. No matter what you tell them, they will at some point chase after the need to feel special.

If you can give it a definition, redirect it, and set them up to **earn** what they already want, you will have saved them years of confusion, embarrassment, self-imposed feelings of inferiority, foolish pursuits and a focus on weaknesses. You will instead have given them an attitude that will serve them for a lifetime.

However, specialness cannot be achieved for life from a single event. It has the property of very soon becoming a thing of the past. A badge earned at fifteen decorates the honour you earned at age fifteen only, not twenty, or twenty-five. To feel special, you ought to be ready and feel ready for all the battles, not just one. Also, 'achievements' does not necessarily mean trophies won in tournaments or contests. Achievements can be personal as well; for example, learning a new language, which has the same consequences of something won on stage. It will give you knowledge, self-belief, useful habits, it will create opportunities and give you status in the eyes of people. Any achievement—personal or public—is a thing of uniqueness. Therefore, making a sandwich or an omelette is not considered as an achievement—although some may beg to differ for the sake of trolling. Even the act of making sandwiches or omelettes every day for the rest of your life cannot be considered an achievement, unless you have the written testimony of world-class sandwich experts that your sandwich is way better than any sandwich made elsewhere, in which case, your sandwich shall be referred to as **the** sandwich, not **a** sandwich, and will be inducted as an achievement.

THIS IS HOW YOU DON'T BECOME SPECIAL

You need to make it completely clear in your mind that others recognising you, giving you attention, a moment of their time, is **not** you being treated as somebody special. You translate that into specialness because you hardly ever feel good about yourself. This means you have never consciously devised a way to make yourself feel better. It's the burden of feeling inadequate in your mind that makes normal acts of kindness from others seem like special acts, which they are not. Guys say, 'You are special', to girls they are trying to have sex with. The point is, if you rely on others to feel special, then that may become the norm in your life, then a habit and, after that, a crippling need. Appreciate their kindness, of course, in cases where there was no motive behind the words. And if there was one, you can appreciate the sentiment, take inspiration from it, if it's work related, and be aware of their motives. Whatever the case may be, the right to feel special must be **earned** and must only be **yours** to give. It shouldn't belong to others because:

- The world might not share their opinion.
- Having practical expectations from the world will make you more self-reliant and less reliant on the good words of others. This will save you from constantly trying to please people and feeling miserable when you fail.
- If you need somebody else to tell you that you are special, then you have not done anything to earn it in your own mind.

OTHERS CAN NEVER MAKE YOU FEEL SPECIAL FOR LONG

There are people who, despite having achieved, learned, and progressed a lot in their lives, have no sense of specialness in their minds. It happens because they did it all to prove something to somebody—it could be their parents, society, teachers. It was fuelled by pressure, competition, culture, and everything else but their own selves. Their lives to this day function on the principle that achievements and better performances are means to please those whom they have deemed gods. *If they are pleased by me, then I am special.*

This is how their lives work:

- *Whatever I do, I do to prove to the world that I can do it.* Basically, to be accepted by the world.

- Soon afterwards, the 'world' is replaced by people who become the ideal models of behaviour and performance, models you look up to. Therefore— *Whatever I do, I must do it better to impress them.*
- The idea then becomes to please them until you *become* them, and have their blessing and assurance that you have become what **they** would like you to be.

If you are living this life, flip the script, which means:

- *Whatever I do, I do it for myself, because I want to prove to myself I can do it*, recognising that whatever you do in turn impacts the world.
- *Because whatever I do impacts the world, I shall and must become better, so I can impact the world for the better.*
- Those who hold prizes, positions and power are sources to learn from—and nothing else. You know nothing about their lives except for their abilities. Admire the fact that they have those abilities, and leave it at that.

When they appreciate you, single you out, congratulate you and welcome your efforts, you must understand that it is a normal, deserved reaction to your praiseworthy actions, not acts of benevolence from higher beings. You can appreciate that treatment, and make sure to in turn pass it on to others. But if you label it as something that makes you special, then that high of feeling special becomes dependent on that pat on the back, a compliment, a word of admiration to feel good about yourself. By doing that, you are silently setting yourself up to be crushed mentally the day you hear the opposite of those words, the day it's not a pat on the back but a backhanded comment, not a compliment but an unpleasant remark, not a word of admiration but a rejection of your performance. This is a relationship between a master and servant, neither of whom is special without the other; the master relies on the servant's presence for his special status, the servant on the master's words of kindness.

The truth about most people who have achieved a lot but depend on the praise of others to feel special is, you are already special. Nobody ever taught you to think from this point of view. Nobody taught you what specialness actually is. And nobody taught the same to those who haven't achieved much either. Specialness, in essence, does not require anybody but the **individual**. One can simply close their eyes and ask themselves, *Why am I special? What have I done in my life?*, and get a clear answer. In case you feel dissatisfied, then you have the option to **earn** it. *Nobody gives it to you, you have to take it.* But that's the hard part, earning it. It is to escape from this answer that we look for specialness in love, appreciative comments, and attention through social media or friends. It is because we know we aren't special in our own eyes, that we at least want to be told by others that we are in theirs. Once you realise this, your specialness is taken away from the approval and acceptance of others and handed exclusively to the self. Specialness then becomes a collection of skills, and feeling special is the sensation felt on upgrading in life after having mastered a skill.

CHAPTER THREE

WHAT REJECTIONS DO TO US

Side note: This is an intro chapter about rejections. We are warming ourselves up for a ride. One of the most important things we are going to do from now on is talk about foundational principles. What the fuck does that mean? Well, it's basically re-considering your perceptions of things, or creating perceptions of things if you don't have any. You get hurt about things and start doing extremely stupid shit because a lot of times you are looking at it the wrong way. Perceptions matter, my friend, the way you look at something matters a lot. If you can see things a certain way, that gives you the ability to avoid pointless suffering from it—why wouldn't you want that! So, without further ado, let's begin.

Rejections are a part of life. You are going to get rejected by those you desire, and you will not always get a fair shot in the competition.

People are motivated by various factors to make decisions to the detriment of your happiness or prosperity. The point is, on many occasions, it won't have anything to do with you. This is a big world we live in, with a lot of people. You're just one of them. And sadly, the world doesn't revolve around you, which kinda leaves you with very bad odds.

Now, because we know rejections are a part of life and happen every single day to somebody, we need to have a way of looking at rejections that helps us overcome them easily, and not be scared into a little hole by them. Our first foundational principle is: Rejections are normal. It might be very late for you to start seeing it in this way because you may have already spent a lot of years being psychologically mauled by rejections, failures and losses. Don't worry, we will talk about everything. For now, start re-writing your perception of rejections of any kind with these three words: rejections are normal.

Rejections are a commonly found species of ancient beasts that get everyone in all fields of life. As mentioned before, it may have nothing to do with you when it happens, but because you are a self-important, self-loving son of a gun, you think from your ego instead of your rational mind and make it all about yourself. You act as if you're the only one it has happened to. Therefore, once again, rejections are normal—start seeing it this way. They happen to everybody.

REJECTIONS DURING TEEN YEARS
ARE THE WORST

Although rejections continue throughout your lifetime, they tend to have a brutal effect in the initial years, a time when you are a little too passionate, too hopeful and a little too entitled. It might have been in your early years of schooling, when a teacher you really wanted to be noticed by somehow always moved past you as if you were an unwanted ad. Or, it could have been a person you liked, or a person with authority or charisma. The sensation felt from that experience was, *Am I invisible to them?* Your mind is unable to come up with any rational explanation for such behaviour from others, and you're too embarrassed to open up to your parents about it. In case you do, chances are they see it as an opportunity to fill your mind with complete nonsense: *Something is wrong with that person for not realising how great you are, so screw that person for not seeing that.*

Of course, your perception can't agree with *screw them,* it goes in direct contradiction to the fact that you like them and wish to be liked by them in return. You have given them value, in your mind. Therefore, what you end up feeling in the absence of a sensible explanation for what is happening is—*Something is wrong with me.*

As time goes by, these sensations double, triple and start to multiply. You haven't been selected for a school activity, a debate, a play, the sports team; the 'cool' senior students don't seem to take a shine to you; and most devastating of all, your crush, the really pretty one or the popular one, those whom everybody seems to be interested in and talks about, doesn't notice you at all either, even though you are crushing it in the contest of staring at them. That's when the voice starts to become louder: *Maybe something **is** wrong with me.* From this, the conclusion your underdeveloped brain draws is: *I am not special.* As discussed earlier, you haven't the slightest clue of what being special means either.

These are the developmental years of the perceptions and personality of a person, and the only tool at hand is an underdeveloped brain. Without guidance, the response to being rejected is rarely going to be mature. A heartbreak, opportunity lost and isolation may make you feel it's the end of the world. So, depending on your fearfulness, fearlessness, strength, weakness, you make a decision about what to do with this voice saying: *I am not special.* In short, you get screwed because you haven't been told that *rejections are fucking normal, mate.* Your mind doesn't really know how to process emotions productively either. The results could be really disastrous.

BEING MOTIVATED BY REJECTION IS NOT REALLY A GOOD IDEA

Of the *many* outcomes of rejections, three of the results could be:

- *I am going to accept that I am a loser.*
- *The world doesn't notice me; therefore, I will become successful to be noticed. I will show them. I will prove to them I am superior/better/above them all, and they are going to regret not choosing me.*
- *I am going to declare that the world is unfair; basically a shitty place, and devote myself to blaming, hating and spreading toxicity.*

You may think the second point is quite powerful—*Kudos to that kid*. Well, not really. That person is going to be successful only so they can prove to **others** that they are a somebody. And, in that pursuit, they will most probably chase success blindly, ignoring what they actually want to do, because their prime motivation isn't to be self-satisfied, but to satisfy **others**. And here's the fatal flaw behind this motivation: the desire to prove something to others requires that these 'others' actually care, which they don't. You are the only one invested in what becomes of you. And the only thing they are interested in, is what becomes of *them*.

Also, in the likelihood that the person choosing option two is not able to achieve that success, what option do they have but to become more bitter, more sad? And let's assume they do achieve that success, what are the chances that these 'others' would be satisfied? What if those you want to prove your superiority to become more successful than you? Should you shave your head out of frustration at this point?

This thinking goes completely against the idea of knowing how to think because, at some point, you will be forced towards introspection by your own mind and age, and such choices and pursuits serve as the prime ingredients for an existential crisis. This may, with time, also create a bitter, meaningless outlook on what you do, because what you have built is a personality that relies heavily on proving itself to others. The self is mostly or entirely clueless, because the mind has been trained to look towards those you respect to give you satisfaction.

Those who are able to find out what they want to do in life chase after greatness to prove to themselves that they are great at what they do. With time, they realise they don't need anybody's approval, as doing what they want to do gives them purpose, and fulfilling that purpose gives them satisfaction and a meaningful life.

CHAPTER FOUR

PEOPLE ARE WEIRD

Side note: We will be talking about our second foundational principle here, which has to do with your general perception of people. Why do we need a general perception for people? Well, because we get rejected by them all the time, and it hurts a lot in many cases. That's what this chapter is about; so hold on to your sweet seatbelts and shift the gears of your reasoning to the maximum as this foundational principle is called: 'People are weird'. Yes, that's how I want you to start seeing people from now on.

WHAT DO YOU THINK OF PEOPLE?

To understand how to deal with something, you need to first figure out what it is you're dealing with. Your understanding of that thing builds a perception of it in your mind, and based on that perception, you build expectations. This is not very complicated; you do this with almost everything. You have strong perceptions about animals—a lion is dangerous, so is a crocodile. And this perception influences your expectations from them. You expect a lion or crocodile to attack you, and therefore you act accordingly. Similarly, a domesticated dog is perceived differently by you, hence your expectations from that animal are friendliness and playful behaviour, and you act in accordance with **those** expectations. Now comes humans: What is your perception of them?

Let's think of a few adjectives you may have heard or used for people: people are stupid, morons, idiots, selfish, untrustworthy, unreliable, calculative, assholes, trash, the list goes on in all spectrums.

There are two problems with the above. One, these are too specific; and two, because they are too specific, you don't really believe them. You have seen people perform acts of amazing selflessness. You have seen, at a professional fighting event, two warriors beat the living crap out of each other, and after the fight, hug each other, congratulate each other and show respect for each other. The theory that people are garbage flies right out of the window after witnessing that.

But you don't believe people are amazing creatures either. You have been hurt, mistreated, wronged, judged and cheated by people. You have heard, read and watched multiple stories of others getting hurt by people. And you have been warned by people you trust to look out for yourself and not blindly believe in people.

In the midst of all of this, what to really think? Are people too complicated? For convenience, one could just leave it at that. Is that what you believe? The truth is, you have never really thought about it. You may say, *People are complicated,* or agree with that because it seems like the most logical answer. That's the difference between 'knowing' and 'understanding'. You *know* a lot of sensible things, but the reason why you don't apply them is because you don't *understand* them. To understand something, it must come from the reasoning of your own mind. Knowledge can be borrowed, but you can't borrow understanding. Once you reach a conclusion derived from your thinking, it is called a realisation. And once you realise something, your perception changes about it once and for all. And that perception remains locked down until another realisation impacts it—that's the process of learning and growing.

YOU ARE CONFUSED

When it comes to people, the right answer is, *I don't know.* You, sir or madam, don't have one perception of people in general, you are confused.

It is entirely possible that there isn't a day when you aren't defining what people are. It could be conversations in which you are giving advice to someone you care about. It could be a discussion on how people think or behave in different situations. It could even be a debate on the state of the world caused by the people in it. And these definitions of people change regularly depending on the context, mood and bias of the individual. People become 'great', if it is a beautiful story warming the heart of the listeners and storyteller. People are 'stupid', when someone you firmly oppose gets elected. People are 'assholes', when someone you trusted screws you over.

So, it's understandable why it must be hard for you to pick one perception of people with conviction, and have it consistently serve you in changing situations.

As mentioned before, you can't put your entire belief in *people are stupid* or *people are amazing*—both are too specific. They don't inspire believability if you want to see people in a realistic way. The one we are left with is, *people are complicated*. The problem with that is, although it is sensible, it isn't personal; it sounds like we are defining machinery we don't know much about. *It's complicated.* It makes people seem more distant, secretive and difficult to understand.

Why not try *people are weird?* Weird is one of the most fantastic words humans have come up with. It is neither a fully positive nor negative term. People on the internet often call themselves weird, almost as if they are paying a compliment to themselves, which shows it has connotations of positivity and self-acceptance in it. At the same time, it has the property of strangeness to it, which gives space for people to act oddly at times. *People act strange 'coz they are weird.* It also has the property of fun, allowing people to act silly without judgement. Lastly, 'weird' has the same sense of mystery that 'complicated' does, but without that wall of impossible penetration.

Let's test all of the above in scenarios involving rejection:

I don't know why they don't want to be friends with me. I guess people are fucking stupid.

It doesn't make sense unless you actually believe they are missing out because you're so amazing and awesome. This would come from self-assumed superiority, arrogance, self-obsession and a disregard for others' opinions when they don't agree with your plans.

She doesn't want to be with me because she is amazing.

This doesn't make sense either, because saying this would be concluding that you are inferior. It involves self-degradation, murder of self-belief, self-esteem and self-worth.

They don't want to be my friends because people are complicated.

It actually doesn't help at all on an emotional level, because the two parts of the sentence feel completely unrelated to each other. One sounds like something that affects you, and the other an unemotional fact.

They don't want to be my friends, because, well, people are weird.

This leaves room for an actual reason to exist which, perhaps, is currently unknown to you. It allows for doubt to fill the space instead of assumptions from ego or hurt. Frankly, you don't have all the facts to make any assumptions, judgements, or conclusions. By saying people are weird, you allow the experience to not affect your ego. *Let it go, man, people are weird; you don't have to understand them, nor blame anyone.* The truth is, you don't have the slightest idea what's going on in their lives, what kind of a person they are, what their motivations are behind forming relationships. You don't know anything about them. You tried, and that's great. Always remember: your job is not to understand people, but to understand and take care of **yourself**.

What we have understood so far is:

- We need a general attitude towards rejections in life, *rejections are normal, they happen.*
- In terms of rejections from people, it becomes: *rejections are a normal thing, and I don't have to take them personally, because people are weird. Who knows what's going on in their heads—it's not my job to find out.*

WHY THINKING PEOPLE ARE WEIRD IS AWESOME

Why is having the perception *people are weird* necessary for your growth?

For one, having a perception to fall back on is better than having no perception at all, and much better than having delusional perceptions. To understand why this perception is better, we have to go back to the statement at the beginning of this chapter. Your perception of something creates expectations from them. Where does this perception come from? In one word, data. Your perception of lions comes from data about lions. They are predators who wouldn't differentiate between a baby and a man in terms of food; they lack empathy, are territorial and fierce hunters. Your expectations come from a perception about lions which is formed by factual behavioural **data** about them.

What about people you want to be friends with or desire romantically? Your expectations from them come from a perception which has **no** real data backing it. You are getting hurt, disappointed and affected by rejections from people you have no data about. What you have is impressions of them, **first impressions** to be precise, which is debatable data, or unreliable data, to say the least. Here's how it happens in your mind, stepwise:

- You notice a person, and you think, *Hmm.*
- The '*hmm*' can be caused by multiple reasons: they are physically attractive, appear to be warm, friendly,

fatherly, kind, intelligent, knowledgeable, mature, wild, fun, crazy and awesome to you.

- These first impressions are registered in your mind, creating an attraction towards them in a friendly way, or a romantic way, or in a purely attention- and approval-seeking way.

- From these first impressions emerge expectations: *I would like to be friends with them, I would like them to take me under their wing, I want them to notice me and like me, I want them to think I am cool, I want them to be mine, I want them to assure me I am capable, I want them to assure me I am sane, fun, valuable, too.*

- These expectations further push the first impressions into conclusions about them in your mind—*they are perfect beings,* or something very close to that.

- This is a very important stage. The truth is, there is no actual data to support all these claims, only impressions created in the first moments of interaction with these people and from what others say or feel about them. Therefore, your response should be: *They may seem this way, but I don't fucking know.* Instead of doing that, your brain starts a brilliant new process called idealisation, which involves your imagination.

- When you start to idealise them, they begin to appear more special to you; you focus more on them and your expectations from them strengthen. You have already accepted without proof or confirmation that they are what your first impressions tell you. Now, you are running scenarios of them accepting you and becoming your friends, and you are making plans with them in your mind.

- You get hurt when none of that happens.
- In case it does happen, in the long run, let's say, after years, you realise they are completely different from what you believed they were. Now they are completely human to you, which means regular, ordinary people with plenty of flaws, insecurities, and unimpressive accounts to their life's story. Your excitement about them is over.
- The process repeats with new people.

BECOME MORE LOGICAL, LESS EMOTIONAL

Here are four concrete points you need to remember very clearly to avoid the above from happening again:

1. Data is king. Knowledge about something, anything, comes from data—remind yourself of this. *I am not going to expect anything from them. I know practically nothing about their life. I am going to observe and wait for real data to show up.* Waiting means that you allow yourself time to calm down from your initial excitement. *I am not going to judge them based on rumours about them, nor buy into the* *hype around them.* There is a possibility that you might not even get real data about them unless you are working closely with them.

Real data is any pattern of behaviour and thought that backs a person's **actions**, not words. People say a lot of shit to sound amazing. The sentiment behind what they say could very well be to sound thoughtful, caring and kind on purpose. But what people say and what they do are quite often two separate things. Therefore, don't outright buy the nice-sounding bullshit they say. **Observe** whether it reflects in their choices as well. Choices, specifically, reveal the thought process of that person because, in making any choice, a person is also rejecting the other available options. Real data is found in the choices they make, not what they say they would like to make. Fuck what they would like to do, focus on what people actually do.

2. First impressions are horseshit. Make a conscious effort to dissolve the first impressions your brain is making of people. First impressions don't come from data, but from how you perceive the world—which relies solely on your level of intelligence and knowledge. So let's talk about your intelligence. Do you have a history of figuring out people accurately? Do you claim it takes you no time to find out who's who? Or do you have a tendency to trust people too soon, forming completely wrong perceptions and ideas about them and realising later it was horseshit?

It is entirely possible you're too hopeful, too naive and a believer in people, a believer in the goodness in people. Two things you need to consider:

- Whoever you are, or however you try to appear in front of people, manipulates your perception of people as well. For example, *I am nice, therefore others must be nice as well.*

- Whatever you believe in does not change the practical reality that people are not you. If you are nice—good for you—that is by no means a guarantee that people will not be themselves.

The point is, do not rely on your intelligence to make assumptions about people if it isn't considering the **practical reality** outside of you. Once you remove those general assumptions that your mind takes for granted, and the first impressions, what you are left with is, *I don't know*—which is the most intellectual place to be in regarding all matters of life.

3. People are fucking weird. With *people are weird in general* as your foundational principle, you avoid falling for the assumptions your mind takes for granted, as well as first impressions. You stop seeing them as impressive, perfect, special beings. They are not. Nobody is. Instead, your outlook is slight uncertainty. You invite caution in your life and a healthy level of scepticism. You keep your trust in the back-pocket, but at the same time you aren't judgemental, negative or dismissive of people. Like we said before, *I am not going to judge them based on rumours, nor am I going to buy into the hype around them. I simply don't know.*

4. We live in a world of marketing, advertising and sales. Anybody can sell you anything—having no real data creates that opportunity. The first impression is bullshit because it comes from a lack of data. Why not entertain the possibility that it is salesmanship until proven otherwise! You don't, because thinking along those lines might feel unkind and unfair. You want to give the other person a chance because you like them from your first impressions. Another reason why you don't consider that somebody might be selling bullshit to you is because of our very ignorant perception of bad people, which comes from an oversimplified division of good and bad.

A bad person, in your mind, is one who is manipulative, calculative, lying, scheming, Machiavellian, sociopathic, or a criminal mastermind, basically somebody who has the word 'bad' written all over them. That's what watching fucking movies and TV shows have taught you. So, you avoid considering that with a person who is making you feel good. What you need to realise is that 'bad' people, basically those who are going to screw you over, unlike in movies and TV shows, don't announce to the world that they are bad. People who are going to be good to you as well as people with self-serving motives or 'bad' motives, both know a single unbendable fact: there is only one route to gaining your trust and coming into your life—by being nice to you and making you feel good. *In the beginning, they were great.* Therefore, until you have **real data**, the perception *'they are weird',* which essentially means, *I don't know them at all,* helps you avoid falling into traps that take years of your life away and teach you nothing new.

The next time you meet someone who forms a great first impression in your eyes, never forget, people are fucking weird. So screw the first impression no matter what they do professionally. Accept that we live in a world of marketing, so screw what they are selling—charm, looks, profundity, it doesn't matter. And always keep an eye out for real data. That is what will end the practice of you thinking that any person who makes you feel good in the beginning is special.

CHAPTER FIVE

DO FAILURES MESS YOU UP?

Side note: If you are an achiever in life, this chapter is not for you. The second chapter about specialness was more than enough. This is strictly for those who are confused, battling the fear of failure, and those who have yet to achieve something. In this chapter, we will expand on the foundational principle *Rejections are normal* in the direction of failure, the fear of failure, and how winning is done.

HOW NOT TO DEAL WITH FAILURE

Rejections are normal. Without a foundational principle on how to see failure and rejection, whenever you don't succeed in something you care about, the first thoughts are: *I am a fucking idiot, I am nothing, I am a loser, I don't deserve anything, I deserve to die.* In many cases, these feelings are accompanied by fear of your parents' wrath, friends' judgement, people's disappointment. *How am I going to tell my parents? Everybody is going to think I am a loser. I am good for nothing because my friends got through. Everybody is going to move on, and I will be stuck here forever.*

Some of the worst outcomes are:

- You become so afraid of failing again that you find excuses to back out and not sign up for any competition, challenge or opportunity with the same risk involved.

- You stick to one place. You don't change your job, as if you have married the workplace. Changing jobs feels like a new challenge; it involves a new environment, new people, new tasks, and the word 'new' brings a strong feeling of uncertainty to you. It's a *maybe* to you—*maybe I will fail there, maybe I will not perform well there, maybe I will have to act differently there, maybe I will have to learn different things there.* And the focus in all those maybes is on the worst possibility: *It won't work out.*

- You convince yourself that you are mediocre. Your mind looks only for safe options now, and your part-time job is to scare other people into looking at the world like you do. *Mediocrity is safe.*

- As a coping mechanism, you treat it as if it's a matter of choice. *I am a cool guy who never studies and always fails in exams, that's my thing.* You think people are laughing with you, when in reality, they are laughing at you, which you only realise once they have all moved on in their lives, and you are left with limited options considering the consistent track record in failing.

This chain of self-harm needs to be broken with the **knowledge** that failures, losses and rejections are normal, and a solution that directs all those highly powerful negative emotions into something useful. To understand that, you need to first understand how winning is done the right way.

HOW WINNING IS DONE MENTALLY

It starts with a question: You wanna do this, right?

This may seem like a very simple question, but, my friend, there is a difference between *wanting* to do something and *having* to do something. Most people in this world are doing what they do not because they want to, but because they have to. Having to do something becomes a duty you have to fulfil. Wanting to do something is a **choice**. Therefore, to win, the very first thing you need to clarify in your mind is, do you really wanna do this?

When it's a choice, there is an ownership of doing that thing. You want to do it. You are not doing it because somebody else is on your ass, you will get fired if you don't, you will have a bad report as an employee—all of these mean you don't care much. You don't mind having fun and stalling the work, because you have the idea that you can do it at the last minute.

Here's a very simple thing, if you don't care, if you don't take what you do seriously, then forget about winning, ever. So, decide right now in your mind, do you wanna fucking do this or not? That's the first step.

One might ask, and quite reasonably so, *Why don't you wait until you have figured out what you want to do, and do that?*

The problem with this question is, it comes with the privilege of being able to afford to **wait**, which a large part of this world can't. The laws that govern their circumstances simply state: you have to do something **right now**.

So, the three possible answers to the question *Do you wanna do this?*, are: *yes, no, I don't know*. The answers, *no,* and *I don't know*, occupy a great many people. The argument they make is, we are not successful because of our **lack of interest** in the thing. *I have no interest in what I do. It doesn't motivate me.* In short, you are not successful because you don't know what to do. This is a highly misplaced argument because it assumes that everybody who is successful must be deeply in love with what they do. That is a quarter of the truth, which means it is 75 per cent bullshit. People are successful for a number of reasons:

- A hunger for money, status, power;
- A hunger to avoid poverty, desperation and conditions you wouldn't want to go back to ever again;
- A hunger to prove in your own eyes that you are capable (which would be the concept of being special);
- A hunger to provide for those whom you love and are dependent on you.

Success is a matter of choice—it doesn't matter what the hunger is. Once you have made that choice, once you have made it a want, we enter the second step: how you see winning.

There are two types of winning that we see in this world: the traditional winning and the real winning.

What traditional winning looks like: this is basically how society crowns a winner. The results of any competition declare a winner and the losers. Society celebrates the winner and ignores the losers—that's the common practice you grew up seeing. Nobody gives a fuck about the loser, so losing becomes a thing to be sad about. The winner is loved and appreciated by all, therefore winning becomes a certification of potential.

How real winning works: one wins after having failed time after time. The essence behind real winning is not giving up, no matter what badges and medals society is handing out. When it comes to your 'heroes' and those who define success and hard work for you, you see them the same way. These people are your heroes because they display an impressive standard of consistent hard work, and through that hard work have achieved expertise in their fields. And that is why you love to fixate on and romanticise how many times they failed, lost and were rejected. You are hugely understanding and forgiving of their failures and mistakes. You believe in them because you know they are not the type to give up.

So, in your story, the traditional sense of winning applies. In the stories of those you admire, winning has everything to do with a never-give-up spirit, excelling in a skill, and doing so by hard work. Why don't you apply the same to **your** story as well?

The only reason why you are still stuck with traditional winning is because you grew up seeing it, and because society treats it as the most important thing. But you won't make it very far with the traditional sense of winning because:

- It's short sighted. It's focused only on an event, the results of an exam, a competition. It appeals to the need for **instant** gratification. *I won this, I won something, now I am important, a winner, and special.* Winning is not a single event, it's a continuing process. There are plenty of people scratching their heads, wondering, *I used to be at the top of my class and now I am nowhere, what happened!* You got happy with those wins and lost track of what comes after and what happened before.

- As long as you feel insanely happy about winning, you're going to feel intolerably miserable with losses. As a result, it might become hard to avoid being permanently afraid and unsure after failure, or become cocky and overconfident after a win.

HOW WINNING IS DONE PRACTICALLY

You want to be special. **This** specialness is not about being superficial, it is about being capable. Earn specialness by becoming capable. Once you have decided to become capable, start seeing whatever you are doing as a **challenge**. The mindset of looking at things as challenges appeals directly to your ego. Whether you feel you are interested in it or not becomes unimportant. Your hunger to become capable is far greater than how the challenges make you feel. Once you have understood and accepted the concept of specialness, your focus deviates from traditional winning.

Real winning requires your focus on neither winning nor losing, but upon **learning**. You start seeing whatever you are learning from the point of view of utility, opportunity and ability. Take whatever you are learning right now, whatever you are currently doing with your life, and ask the questions below from these three points of view.

Utility asks you: what's the use of what you are learning? In how many areas, fields of study and practices can it be implemented? How much self-belief does this learning generate in you? How much self-value does it provide? Does it have value in the long term, in the market? And lastly, at what point does whatever you are learning start to have real utility in terms of success? Basically, where do you stand right now? Thinking in terms of utility makes you realise that there is a real world out there, away from your frog-well, with real competition, and the trophies you may be collecting are mere indicators that you are on the right path, but you haven't actually won.

Opportunity asks you: how can you use what you are learning? How many doors will it open for you? In how many ways can you capitalise on this skill? How many opportunities does it have in the marketplace? What's the full potential of this skill if learned until you are an expert? Where is the geographic hub for opportunities for this skill? Thinking in terms of opportunity gives you ambition. Ambition gives you seriousness. With ambitious goals, the nature of its utility in your mind is revised and reset as well.

Ability asks you: how well can you do what you are learning? Do you have a natural talent for this? Are you able to learn this faster than others? Are you slower than others? If yes, then despite being slower, are you able to beat the competition or stand on par by working harder than them? Success cares about nothing but results. Are you able to think creatively, which means can you create new opportunities from the existing ones? Are you able to think cleverly? Thinking in terms of abilities makes you aware of where you stand right now and where your ambition requires you to be standing.

Once you start seeing winning from these points of view, you get clarity and a vision. Now we move to the third step: how to see failures.

HOW REAL WINNERS SEE FAILURES

Make the fact that *failures, rejections and losses are normal* a **foundational** principle upon which your brain works. Real winning is a journey. Despite knowing this, people tend to give up the entire prospect of winning at the first sight of failure. One of the big reasons is that, in your mind, you have certain qualifiers. They could be getting into this college, gaining that skill by a specific time, reaching there or becoming this at a certain age. These are deadlines and milestones in your plan that you **have to** achieve to give yourself enough believability that you can pull this off. And once you fail in one of those things, you give up the entire venture altogether.

The truth is, there is a huge possibility that you're going to fail a lot, again and again, in almost all of those qualifiers. The reason why you need to stop taking them so seriously is because they are coming from **your mind,** which tells you how things should happen, **not reality,** which shows you how things actually do happen.

When the plan isn't working, whatever negative conclusions you may draw also come from your mind. You need to understand that these failures can only change the path of the journey, not the direction. For example, if you wanted to get a degree, but you're upset because it's not going to be from the prestigious university you hoped to get into, then you're still stuck with the traditional mindset of winning. Focus on **learning**, which would suggest that you get a degree from wherever that subject is taught. As long as you're alive and functioning, the chance of getting back on top and amongst the greatest **exists.** It depends exclusively on your own dedication to build **masterful** skills in it. If you decide that you want it, then nobody can stop you. The only downside of failing is that your path may become longer, but you're not dying in the next five years. You have the time, so focus on building that skill no matter where you are.

And that's how winning is done, it's not about which college you went to, which trophies you won at age fifteen; it's about where you stand, what your capabilities are, and what you can show when the opportunities come. Success depends entirely on your preparation. So believe that it's going to be a journey, and there are going to be plenty of failures, and that's all right. But at the end, you win by becoming too good to be ignored.

FAILURES TEACH YOU HOW TO WIN THE WAR

Once you have adopted '*failures are normal*' as the foundational principle in real winning, when you fail, you do not emotionally punch yourself. Your emotions are focused less on feeling miserable and more on conducting an investigation. You recognise that, although **failures are normal**, that does not mean they are nothing. Real winning requires the minimisation of losses to the best of your control.

What is the investigation?

First, you take ownership of the failure. It's very different from acting as if you have been stung by failure. Both are similar realisations, but come from different points of view. The first makes you responsible, the other a victim. Instead of finding tendencies, people and relationships to blame, you make **yourself** fully responsible for that failure. This is step one of the investigation. *I deserve this. Whatever impact this failure causes, I deserve and take responsibility for it.* Once you take ownership, it becomes **your** fuck-up. You are not a victim, it didn't **happen** to you, **you caused it**. Once you **own** it, everything before that failure comes into scrutiny, all those people, relationships and tendencies that could have taken the blame; they all have to go under the surgeon's knife.

After ownership begins assessment: *Why did I fail?* Assessment produces findings about your abilities, habits, relationships and the people in your life. For example, what was your approach going into the competition—serious or lazy? Did your approach include following a plan, routine, daily rituals backed by strict discipline? Or was it just counting the months left and convincing yourself of bullshit like you've still got it under control? If your approach was serious, then should you have worked for more hours a day? What state of mind did you have the entire time? Was your focus clouded by emotional entanglements? Were you busy in the consumption of short-term pleasures? Or were you desperately running after getting laid or finding true love?

Whatever your findings are, for the sake of success, you learn and incorporate them into your life as changes to be made. If you want success, there are going to be huge adjustments, and current relationships will have to go through negotiations. The findings might tell you that certain relationships aren't even deserving of negotiations. They need to go. You need to take back control of your life. You need to recognise the mistakes and readjust your approach and mindset fully and immediately to avoid failures in the future to the best of your control. And this is why failures are important—they teach you everything you need to win the war.

CHAPTER SIX

FINDING LOVE CAN BE A PAIN IN THE ASS

Side note: In this chapter, we're gonna talk about rejections from those we desire romantically. Of course, this will be done while keeping in place our foundational principle, Rejections are normal. We are going to be talking about how to find the right person, how to avoid dating the wrong people, and probably almost everything else relationship-related. Let's see how we fare in this journey of ours. Here we go.

WHY DID THEY REJECT ME?

Now, after reading a little you may think, is this chapter just for guys? Nope. But it is very important to address specifically what teenage guys learn from rejections. Once that's done with, it's everybody we are talking about.

The first rejection from people you like tends to happen at a very young age, let's say around ten. At that time, you might think a combination of a few things:

- An inspection into self: *I am poor, I am not cool, I am not good-looking, I am way cooler.*
- An inspection of the systems concerned: *Dating is stupid, feelings are stupid, love is stupid.*
- An inspection of the sex involved: *Girls are stupid, guys are stupid, guys are clueless, guys don't know what they want, girls are complicated, what do girls want, I don't understand them, nobody can understand them.*

The point is, our observations at that age are simple and not very impactful.

But, as you grow older, rejections become more hurtful, which puts a greater emphasis on the question: *Why did they reject me?* Your brain answers: *They want something I don't have,* which—although accurate—still does not answer, *What is it that I don't have?* And this opens the gates to theories.

Straight teenage guys tend to receive information like: *They want money, free transportation, expensive dates, gifts, excitement which comes from an expensive lifestyle, muscles, height, sex, perfect facial symmetry, popularity, rude behaviour, lies, jerks, rough sex, big dicks, fun, dumb guys,* etc. This is what the mind of a teenager gets exposed to when trying to understand and find out why girls are not dating him! And the sources to this 'knowledge' are:

- Dumb friends of the same age.
- Older guys, with age being the only credibility behind their information.

- Anecdotal evidence from guys who were cheated on and left for somebody better.
- Guys with a sales pitch regarding why having sex and ditching girls is the best lifestyle because girls by nature are untrustworthy and confused creatures.
- Watching some girls around them making choices to cheat and choose specifically richer or physically wholesome guys, and having random sexual escapades from time to time, and because such choices are so bold, they capture all the attention, muting the actions of girls who aren't doing that.
- People on the internet opportunistic enough to realise and capitalise on the insecurities, frustration and lack of knowledge of guys who got rejected or left by some girl. And because their business model runs on their customers feeling frustrated, they make sure it doesn't go away. Therefore, they push you further towards victimhood, as you already feel a sense of having been wronged; instead of healing the wound, they deepen the hurt by making sure you don't forget how you were wronged by a girl; and furthermore, they sell ideas or courses on how to become a man, a jerk, a bad boy who will from now on get any woman he wants. In short, what happened will never happen to you again. However, what they teach has no basis in understanding women or people in general from different perspectives; it is highly

short-lived; and it takes you further away from the possibility of building fruitful relationships with women. After all, they care about their profit more than your personal growth.

And since most rejected, confused teenage boys hear and notice all this, the generalisations are convenient and easier to believe. Therefore, in cases where the *why did they reject me* is not clearly stated, one gravitates towards conclusions from the above to cope with the rejection. After all, blaming something is much easier than applying common sense.

YOU ARE STUPID AS FUCK IN YOUR TEENAGE YEARS

What you need to understand is:

- In your teenage years, the brain is underdeveloped; basically, you are stupid as fuck.
- Because you are stupid as fuck, you are gathering information about love, romance, and relationships from movies, television shows and the internet, all of which are selling what you **want to see**.
- You don't know you are stupid as fuck because you think you are an adult. You think that because, to you, your brain is functioning properly to the best of your knowledge, and also because, legally, an

adult means somebody who is eighteen years old—which is absolute fucking nonsense. You remain considerably dumb until twenty-five to twenty-six. That's when adulthood actually begins—adulthood meaning the development of sensibility.

- Because you think of yourself as an adult, you fail to see the girls are as stupid as fuck too, which they are because they are teenagers or in their early twenties as well.

- Because you fail to realise that these girls are not adult beings, your theories on girls become your views on women in general.

- And because these views on women appear as core realities and 'women psychology' to you, the answers for *why I get rejected* drop a hydrogen bomb on your self-esteem. From all of this, rejection from women can cause you to conclude: *To get girls, I will have to become a jerk, an asshole, a playboy, a fuckboi,* or whatever the new term is, *and that is the* only *reason why I am unable to get a girlfriend.*

WE ARE MOSTLY SURROUNDED BY MORONS AS WELL

The truth is, you are confused, hurting from the rejection, and still can't stop thinking about that person. What you ought to be looking for is perspectives on your situation.

Now comes another huge problem: **How to correctly seek help**. To a lot of people, even though this is a matter of great personal importance, seeking help is seen as a weak option. Your ego doesn't allow you to openly seek help regarding rejection out of a fear of exposing your vulnerabilities. Therefore, what you rely on is unsolicited advice.

What does that mean?

It's somebody giving you advice because they have heard you're going through some shit. They have no actual data or details about your problem, just an idea. The problem with unsolicited advice is that it lacks the seriousness required to solve your problem. Firstly, in order to actually solve your problem, a person would have to have a helpful perspective. Secondly, they would require personal details about you to figure out an appropriate solution for you that addresses what you want, the reality of the world, and the bullshit you might be telling yourself.

A person giving you unsolicited help ignores almost all of this. They give you information that is based on what *they* think, what they want to do, and what they probably do. They are mostly interested in how their advice makes them look like in your eyes. Their focus is on the impression they are making, not the solution. They might actually not even care, because the gravity of the situation has not been communicated to them. So, unsolicited advice, more often than not, turns out to be useless.

Your loved ones, on the other hand, are even worse; chances are they might say, *You are special, you will get a better girl/boy next time.* And even if nobody says that to you, your own mind will lead you to it after a while. After all, we refuse to accept we don't deserve the best for ourselves in the spirit of self-importance. Your friends might also slander the person who rejected you: *They didn't deserve you. I never liked them. I always had a bad feeling about them.* To make you happy, they will denigrate the person who rejected you and raise you to sainthood. They bullshit, which is why these statements don't really make sense to you on a personal level. The truth is, the reason why you liked that person is because they are special in your mind; and you remain hurt because they don't like you back.

We don't often get many insightful, helpful perspectives from people around us. Those who do are lucky. So, instead of only focusing on how to deal with rejections, we should look at the source of the problem: What are the influences that shape your ideas of the kind of person you want to date, and the kind of relationship you want? If we can sort out the sources of our expectations, then maybe we can save ourselves from this self-repeating cycle of bad relationships, falling for the wrong people, and getting hurt by rejections.

YOU ARE BEING BULLSHITTED EVERYDAY

In the absence of perspectives, a criteria and foundational principles, what you are learning comes from garbage sources only meant to appeal to your fantasies. These sources include endless streams of movies, TV shows, content creators who qualify as reality TV actors, traditional celebrities, models, vloggers, lifestyle bloggers, YouTubers, Instagram influencers, pop stars, and this star and that star on whichever fucking two-bit app you spend your time on. Their objective is not to teach you or talk about the harsh realities of life. Their objective is to provide entertainment, set unachievable standards and get you hooked on a lifestyle that you cannot afford nor sustain. And this is why you watch them and simultaneously compare your life to theirs: *I wish my life was like that.*

We are living in the age of modern advertising in which **humans** are the products. When you buy, you are buying who they are, how they live, who they date, who their friends are, what they wear and what they do. You want a relationship like the one you saw in a movie. You want a girlfriend like the guys you follow online have. You want friends like those people you watch on YouTube have. You want a lifestyle like the people you follow on social media. You want pictures like the couple you follow on Instagram. You want your boyfriend to do cute things like that YouTuber's boyfriend does, because to you, they seem real. All of it seems real.

You want the truth? They know what you like. It is because they know what you like that they have millions and millions of followers, which earns them millions of dollars. You are **one** of the millions of followers they have. They don't know you. Your **reality** is not a movie. Girlfriends from movies don't fucking exist, which is why they are called fictional characters. Your friends are not going to be a group of extremely good-looking people who have funny things to say every five seconds. You cannot have that lifestyle because such lifestyles do not exist. What exists is the fact that you love watching fantasy. That lifestyle is as real as *Lord of the Rings*. Those gorgeous photographs have been Photoshopped, chosen over hundreds of frames of the same bullshit idea that they want to sell you.

Your boyfriend exists **in** reality, not **for** a manufactured reality in which your relationship is scripted, choreographed and edited for people to watch. You know **nothing** about their reality. Therefore, stop comparing yourself to people you have never met and have no real data about.

The most dominant idea in your mind after having been recruited to support these online products is that you deserve to have the kind of life they do. You think so because you are an emotional fool. Unless you can detach yourself from emotions or control your emotions, you will remain an emotional fool; it takes years to become emotionally intelligent. So, these people become your sources of acquiring knowledge about love, relationships, dating, socialising, lifestyle and self. And your demands are now assumptions of what will make you happy based on what you have been **told** makes others happy. For example, for guys, one such demand is the girls they see online, girls hanging around the internet celebrities you think are your *bros, buddies and family.* The catch is: they are unbelievably attractive in every single frame of the video. You are fascinated by how they dress, their makeup, their bodies. It is this nonsense that gives birth to the idea of the fantasy girlfriend or fantasy partner that you want to have in your life. You have been told, shown and convinced that it **exists**.

And this becomes your criteria for a future partner: that fantasy person. And just like that, you detach yourself from reality, realistic possibilities, realistic outcomes, your shot at stability, your shot at maximum personal development, and in many cases your shot at a great career, your shot at self-awareness, and your shot at evading and minimising traumatic experiences.

YOU ARE CHASING AFTER A FANTASY PERSON

Since millions and millions of people are chasing a fantasy in the real world, what we have are millions of delusional people who are playing fantasy characters, which is taking them farther away from who they really are. Without any introspection or strong belief in their fantasy persona, they can't wrap their heads around why they can't meet that person they are meant to be with; why does every person they date end up being a jerk, cheater, liar, asshole, uncaring, boring, different, controlling, or manipulative at the end. *I mean, what the fuck is wrong with people!* Everything is wrong with you. You are a delusional fool who keeps deciding to date fantasy characters. And despite the rejections or bad relationships, that does not stop. There are only two outcomes from these fantasy relationships: after a course of time, either they are going to be assholes to you, or you are going to be that way to them, precisely because relationships are a thing of reality, not fantasy.

Since we are on the subject of the fantasy partner, let's review your choices: from all your rejections, the messages you didn't get replies to, the requests that weren't accepted, the people you were instantly attracted to, was there ever a variety in these pursuits? Or did all these people fill the same condition of being that fantasy person? The conditions for fantasy girlfriend being:

- She has a great dress sense and hairstyle.
- She looks hot in her pictures.
- She seems to be able to form full sentences with practically no grammatical errors, which is an indication that she is smart.

- And, most importantly, how her body looks from different angles, seated or standing.

Your fantasy is equal parts porn, re-creations of movie scenes of dates and social activities, and of course the assumption that this person will never leave you.

The most common conditions for fantasy boyfriend are:

- He looks presentable and is attractive.
- He is doing something in his life that makes him appear competent.
- He forms full sentences with practically no grammatical errors, which is an indication that he is smart.
- He charmingly challenges you, which creates excitement, unpredictability and the desire to win his approval.

Your fantasy is equal parts clever male protagonists from movies, relationship dynamics from movies, and the assumption that you're the special one for him—which he will convince you that you are, and then use that validation to make you compromise your principles for whatever ideas he has.

This happens commonly with both guys and girls who are playing fantasy characters and wanting to date fantasy characters—whatever your silly influences are. And when the same guys get dumped by these fantasy girls, they struggle to understand why. Well, she found a better fantasy character. What happened was that, over time, your relationship entered reality, which means, to her, you became boring, repetitive and real, just like her actual life. And none of that is movie-like at all.

PICK-UP ARTISTS ARE HUMAN GARBAGE

When rejections like this continue to happen, frustration, anger and hurt accrue in your mind, accompanied by doubt about your own self. At that moment, instead of asking yourself, *What am I running after?* You ask, *Why am I unsuccessful at getting girls?* Still no self-awareness, but plenty of motivation to keep going at it.

At this stage, enter dating gurus and pick-up artists. These are people who have suffered equal or more rejections than you, some of which impaled their egos so much that it forced them to make 'getting girls' a quest in their lives to prove to themselves they are 'the man'. They usually like to refer to themselves as 'alphas' to massage their highly sensitive egos, which also acts as their G-spot during sex. What it means is that they climax immediately upon hearing a girl refer to them as alpha or its variations, such as master, daddy, which basically means they are their father. This is nothing but a crippling need to be validated by an impressionable girl with daddy issues living in a fantasy world. And these guys desperately require the reiteration of the terms alphas, master or daddy **from girls** to compensate for the rejections **by girls** in their past.

From that, you can naturally see how they never fully recovered from their past rejections, and now are teaching **you** how to recover from your rejections by becoming like them, which means as pathetically obsessed with girls as they are—because it's somehow a competition now, *and you need to win.*

What they teach you is that there is absolutely nothing wrong with the type of person you are choosing; on the contrary, you are right to do that. This becomes a reinforcement to choose the same **type** of girls that resemble your fantasy girlfriend. After learning this, instead of questioning your choices, you become more and more enthused to chase after the same type, because now, hope has arisen in you. The doubt which could have benefitted you by making you step towards a realistic analysis of your choices is now erased by the **idea** that you could be with those girls one day. After all, these type of girls are your fantasies, why wouldn't you be biased towards believing you can have them! And that alone causes the delay in finding who you are, because you have now enrolled yourself into becoming somebody you are not.

REJECTIONS MEAN JACK-SHIT

How should you **sensibly** see rejections from those you desire?

The truth is, you don't have **real** data on why you got rejected. In the absence of any data, you let your insecurities fill in all the reasons why you got rejected. What you're supposed to do is, leave it at: *you don't have any real data.* You don't know why. Stop making it personal because you have nothing better to do. You don't know the nature of their wants, **why** they want what they want, their influences, degree of intelligence, degree of experience, who they think they are, who they actually are, and if they know who they actually are. You don't have any data. Therefore, rejection from people should mean jack-shit to you.

Have you ever rejected someone romantically? Even if it required as little effort as swiping your finger, think of how much thought and time went behind it. What were the parameters you were considering behind accepting or rejecting? How stupidly vague, impersonal, and shallow were those parameters? That's how much thought goes behind rejecting someone. Not much. How can you take a rejection personally when it doesn't take more than a few seconds to happen? Do you think your whole existence can be understood, judged and adequately summarised in a matter of seconds? Fuck, no!

Being rejected by someone is not a statement on you. You have no data, you cannot have that data. For you to know, you would have to be able to read their minds. There is a possibility that they have no idea what they are looking for in a relationship and from a partner; they are probably just following their instincts. Or let's say they do know what they're looking for: there is a possibility they have no idea whether it is good for them or not. What matters is, do **you** know what you are looking for? And more importantly, whatever you are looking for—do you know with certainty that it is good for you?

HOW TO LOOK FOR THE RIGHT PERSON

Who are you?

The answer to this decides what type of person you would want to bring into your life. The truth is, the more you know yourself, the more power you have to make a better choice. After all, you can employ that knowledge about yourself—*What kind of a person would be best suited for who I am*—and then look for only such people.

Now, in all fairness, nobody expects you to know yourself a hundred per cent. You're changing with time and experiences, and discovering new things about yourself. So, to make even a half-decent choice, the answer to 'who are you' should be somewhere between where you are right now and where you want to be; in short, somewhere between reality and aspiration. That would be the ideal situation.

What's the reality? Most people have no idea nor any inclination to find out who they are. What they have is either a completely crazy idea about themselves—a fantasy character—or an aspirational idea about themselves which doesn't take practical reality into account.

An example of the first type is, *I am a fucking stud*: this moron thinks he is no less than James Bond and girls should be dying at his feet. Another example is, *I am a queen*: this moron thinks she is royalty or one of the members from the Kardashian clan. The problem is, a lot of people really believe their fantasy characters. And because they believe in them so much, they are working on making them real on a daily basis.

An example of the second type is, *I am a genius at what I do, and the world will one day know about me:* these are people who are so detached from their practical reality that even though they are absolute shit in what they do, instead of accepting their current reality, they think the opposite.

Now, imagine what kind of partners such people would be looking for? They have no self-awareness, so what they look for is either attraction or validation of the bullshit they tell themselves. *I deserve the hottest person. I deserve a really rich guy. I deserve a person who will blindly believe in me.*

When rejected, people who live in a fantasy world think their fantasy character needs more work. *I am not tall, I am not muscular, I am not charismatic, I don't look like that famous person, I don't look like that model on Instagram, I don't have that body yet. I am less, inadequate and undeserving until I have these things.*

When people who think they are the best get rejected, they simply blame the person. *She is dumb. She doesn't get art. He was not intellectual. He was not on my level anyway. He wasn't smart enough.*

If you want a decent relationship, then you need to quit the bullshit of finding these fantasy people, the incredibly hot girl, or the guy from the movies who is always around. You need to be realistic. What you are looking for should be based on who you are right now and where you want to be.

When you start to care about 'who you are' in a realistic manner, instead of blindly falling for people, you start caring about **who they are**. Attractiveness should only be an entry-level qualification; it shouldn't be a deciding factor. There are millions of attractive people on this planet.

So, the first question is, who are you?

This means who you are intellectually, sexually, emotionally and professionally. You can take all the time you want to figure out the first three, and it is up to you to do it. Nobody can do it on your behalf while you sleep.

The last part is who you are professionally, which you can find out by asking these questions:

- *What is my ambition?* (What do you want to become exactly? Where do you want to reach?)
- *What are my current goals?* (Short-term and long-term goals to actualise the ambition mentioned above.)
- *What is the routine I need to achieve my goals?* (Doesn't need explanation.)
- *What are my dreams?* (Why do you want to achieve that?)
- *What is the nature of the line of work I have chosen?* (How demanding is it? What's the scope for relaxation? At what age and with what skillset would you have achieved credible respect in your field or workplace?)

The questions above give you an idea of where you are and where you want to be.

Now you ask the other person the same question, who are you?

The first answer they will naturally go to is what they do, for example, *I am an engineer.* The second answer is whatever gives them an emotional or/and intellectual identity. They might cite race, religion, nationality, belief systems, ideologies, causes, etc. The third answer is the most important. It is data that deals with their choices, decisions and actions, to which you must pay serious attention. What they do as a career doesn't matter. What they say they believe in doesn't fucking matter. How attractive they are means shit. It is what they have done and have been doing that shows you who they are.

Therefore, what you look for is:

- Do the choices, decisions and actions they have made in their past and are making in the present ensure the safety and support of your current purpose in life?
- What patterns do you notice when looking at what they have done and have been doing?
- Do these patterns suggest an approach of carelessness, destructiveness, impulsiveness or of seriousness, self-control and an attempt at stability?

This approach ends your previous experiences with rejections as you aren't focused anymore on people that fascinate you with their appearance and popularity. On the contrary, you are now engaged, silently or vocally, in rejecting people whose decisions, choices and actions seem either incompatible to yours, or disagreeable to you. Not only does this bring down the number of rejections by a **lot**, the impact the rejections have almost stops mattering to you. You're not playing the game of probability anymore. You are not desperately waving your flag to be accepted by anyone you desire. No, you have put the priorities of your own life on top. If you do find such a person but are met with rejection, the reminder that *rejections are normal* applies very aptly in that situation, as you must not forget, *People are weird. It has nothing to do with you.* What you have right now is a criteria, which is much better than having no criteria, and certainly far better than chasing fantasy.

CHAPTER SEVEN

HOW YOUR SELF DIES

Side note: It is entirely possible that you may be slightly exhausted from reading the last chapters. But here's news for you, the chapters from now on are very interesting. So you need to get that energy back up. We are moving to new foundational principles like: fuck approval, acceptance and happiness. It is going to an interesting read. This chapter is a short introduction to our discussion about seeking approval.

THE WARNING

Imagine at the crucially transformative age of thirteen, on one random day, your dad, mom, grandad, or somebody else you trusted sat you down and told you they want to have an important talk with you about avoiding something people do a lot, and you are going to do as well. No, it's not smoking or drugs. Here's what it is.

'Listen up kid, as you grow into adulthood, you're gonna meet a lot of people you will really like. And because you like them, you will really want to be liked by them. Which is fine. It's natural to want to be liked by people you think are great. But there is a thing called approval, which you haven't thought about. It's a very dangerous thing, and if you want to be intelligent, you must never forget it.

'When does it start and how does it work?

'Well, it starts with you wanting to prove to yourself that you are capable. But there are two problems with that. The first problem is, you are a kid. As a kid, you look toward authority to give you confirmation on whether you are good at something or not. Just like in an exam, even if you know you have done very well, you still wait for the teacher to give you that confirmation. You don't get any satisfaction from simply knowing it yourself. Basically, you don't know how to grade yourself yet, so people you see as capable become that authority; you rely on them—and not on yourself—to tell you that you are capable and worthy. To prove you are capable to yourself, you start doing whatever they will like. After all, their approval means you are capable. Your inner voice becomes secondary, their voice becomes everything.

'The second problem is, although you want to prove to yourself you are capable, you don't know what to do in life yet. You're a kid, you haven't figured out shit about what you want. So you look at those who you think are awesome and capable, and whatever they are doing becomes a very practical thing to do to be capable too.

'And just like that, kid, you start doing two things: first, whatever you think will make them like you more. That becomes anything that will please them. Second, because these people are liked or respected, you want to do the exact things they are doing in life, basically replicate their careers. For example, take all the kids who decide to become doctors because their parents are doctors, only to later realise they don't actually wanna be doctors themselves.

'This could either go very well for you or very badly, either way, you won't become intelligent—perhaps smart, even clever, but not intelligent—because that's the path of the follower, not a free person. Do you wanna be intelligent? Then always remember that, whenever you like somebody, there is a thing called "approval", and it can destroy the individual in you.'

THE MURDER OF INDIVIDUALITY

Let's take an example: Think of the last time you felt a deep sense of self-satisfaction from doing something. But once it was presented to the relevant authority—teacher, boss, mentor—they were not very impressed. In fact, they thought it was mediocre. Or they did not show any particular delight or excitement in your creation. And that work, to you, immediately became shitty. It slightly broke your heart, and what once made you proud quickly became something that reminded you of failure.

When such experiences happen, the following changes are made by you:

- You decide to not focus on the feeling of self-satisfaction anymore. There cannot be any satisfaction if it has not been approved by those you want to impress. Satisfaction now comes **after** their approval. What the self says doesn't matter anymore. Only what **they** say matters.

- You stop relying on yourself and rely completely on 'those who know better' to tell you what you should do, how to do it, and what's best for you. Your original ideas don't matter until they have been approved by them.

- Your 'self' is not being developed. It is being ignored and treated as an unreliable entity. What is being fully developed is an identity that you think will be liked by those you want to impress.

- You start working in the direction that will make them happy and which they approve of, instead of finding out what will make **you** satisfied.

The result is, after a period of time, you become completely divorced from your 'self'. What you hear from your self are whispers of what you'd like to do. Those are whispers because the voice of your self has been suppressed so strongly for a very long time. The whispered ideas have no credibility because they have never been trusted or applied.

In short, for a very long period of your life, you remain confused, clueless and always looking for guidance—either for examples you can replicate, or somebody to hold your finger and walk with you.

You are noticing the word 'self' here. The 'self' is the individual in you. It is the person you don't want to accept and run away from to become a different person. It is who you really are. It is who you are meant to know better, empower and develop. And since you're not in touch with your 'self', our first objective would be to unite you with it. Then we will eradicate the parasitical thoughts and practices, like constantly seeking approval and acceptance, which destroys your individuality. One by one, we are gonna deal with everything. Let's start with happiness for now.

CHAPTER EIGHT

SCREW HAPPINESS

HAPPINESS IS YOUR OBJECTIVE

Generally, in life, what you want is happiness. Behind most of your actions, choices and relationships, the demand is happiness. What you haven't realised is that happiness is not the same as **satisfaction**. If you were simply asked, 'Do you feel satisfied with your life?', your mind will look for the answer either elsewhere or someplace deeper than where happiness resides. *I may feel happy, but I don't know if I am satisfied.* It's a question that makes people really pause for a moment and think: *Hmm, never really asked myself that.*

So, what makes you happy?

The general answer to what makes you happy would be, *making my parents happy, being nice to people, partying, smoking weed, watching great television shows and movies that make me think, spending time with my friends, shopping, having sex, working out, watching my favourite content creators, and doing well in life.* Now, ask yourself, does any of that provide you satisfaction? Thinking about this might be hard and challenging for you because, frankly, you have never really thought about self-satisfaction. When something is not on your mind, you obviously don't notice it nor pay attention to it. So you don't think about self-satisfaction because all your attention is focused on happiness. And when happiness is the objective behind your choices and decisions, your mind assesses things you want to do only on the basis of happiness. *Would this make me happy?*

WHAT IS SELF-SATISFACTION?

Your major struggle in life is to be happy; it is not to be satisfied. Now, self-satisfaction does not mean you won't be happy, nor does it mean that you will be happy all the fucking time. What it offers is something better—a state of mind called peacefulness. You would be at peace with yourself. And this is also where the problem comes: to be at peace with yourself, you will have to know your 'self' first. So, how much do you know your self? The answer in a lot of cases would be, fuck-all, because in our youth we are busy practising to become Mr Savage and Ms Flawless. And our 'self', to us, is definitely not those things; it's confused, vulnerable and emotionally unstable. So, we ignore it. What you don't realise is: you can't be something you're not. At best, what you're gonna be is a copy, an imitation and a poor parody. But what you do have is the power to find out who you are, and fix and develop whatever you think is weak.

1. *Self-belief*

The more you know your self, the stronger your belief in 'self' becomes. Yes, the knowledge of self produces self-belief; who knew, right? It happens because, with more and more knowledge, you're able to make better assessments.

What do you think happens when you know nothing about your self? You are either filled with self-doubt or make bad assessments. An example of bad assessment is overconfidence. An overconfident person is one who has badly assessed the information about their own capabilities.

It's as simple as this: you are unsure and scared of what you don't know; you're confident and comfortable with things you know. You experience self-belief because you are getting to know who you are.

2. *What does your self want?*

With knowledge of self comes clarity on **what the self wants**. This is very different from what you want. You can tell yourself thousands of things that you want. What the self wants comes only by knowing the specific wants that make sense to the self.

3. *What you don't want!*

Furthermore, the knowledge of self produces the **knowledge of what you don't want,** which is far more important than knowing what the self wants.

A lot of times in your life, you have no idea if you really want to do something, but you may do it out of impulsiveness or pressure from people around you. Bad habits tend to start this way. A lot of bad experiences happen this way. The logical side of your brain knows it is wrong, but overexcitement or the need for approval takes over. Knowledge of what you don't want interferes and acts as a reminder of what really matters to your 'self'. In moments of confusion, it helps lift you out of the spell of emotional captivation and makes you think logically. When given power, it can become a tool that eliminates anything that will bring harm to the 'self'. For example, in dating, when you know for certain what you don't want, you'd be able to easily run away at the first sight of a red flag.

Therefore, knowing well what your 'self' doesn't want improves your decision-making abilities. This enables your view of yourself as an **individual**, and it also gives your identity uniqueness in the eyes of people.

4. *What makes your self happy?*

Lastly, the knowledge of self also provides the outline and understanding of **what would make the 'self' happy.**

How is this different from whatever you think makes you happy right now? Well, there are a lot of things that make you happy in general—let's call these activities general happiness. The problem with general happiness is, these are things that almost every person in this world enjoys. These activities and things are designed to make people happy. Things that make you happy in general, and things you specifically enjoy, are two different experiences.

There are a lot of things that you might be doing for fun which you don't actually enjoy. You just never cared to listen to that feeling. You're either doing them because other people in this world are doing them, or because people you like are doing them—they are popular or they are what your friends are doing. The truth is, you haven't asked yourself honestly if you actually enjoy this. Knowing what you actually enjoy is one part of knowing what makes the self happy. The other part is knowing what would give you long-lasting happiness. And that has very little to do with enjoyment and more to do with stability and structure in life, thus creating peacefulness in the long run.

So, as a recap, what makes you happy is, one, doing things that are generally known to make people happy, and two, having theoretical ideas and fantasies regarding what would make you happy in the future.

What makes your self happy is knowing **clearly** what activities give you joy, and what would give you satisfaction in the long run.

WHY DO WE CHASE AFTER HAPPINESS LIKE JUNKIES?

The honest answer is because it feels good. And that's why we are trying to find deep, spiritual and mystical secrets behind being happy, relaxed, calm, comfortable and cheerful all the time. We are fucking idiots, that's what we are.

The truth is, life doesn't revolve around happiness. Life is a lot of things that have nothing to do with happiness. But we think it does, because happiness feels fucking great. It's just the best. So, whatever makes you happy, whatever makes you feel good, is what you want. And whatever doesn't and stops making you happy is what you don't care about anymore. We are happiness-junkies. People have left long, stable relationships or cheated on their partners because they met someone new who excites them—that's how much of a happiness-junkie people can be.

The problem with responding more to feeling good is that chances are you may become a person who just focuses on feelings rather than thinking. And thinking is the only thing that will ensure you don't fuck up your life. Ideally, an intelligent person would be one who is more thinking-based than feeling-based.

Feeling-based sounds something like: *This makes me feel good, therefore this is good. I want it.* Thinking-based sounds like: *Just because something makes me feel good doesn't mean it's good. I will think about if I really want it.*

A feeling-based person is impulsive, excitable, lacks a thoughtful process, doesn't take the future into consideration, and is therefore easily defeated by their own feelings and easily manipulated by those who can create nice feelings in them.

A thinking-based person is one who considers stability, the future, the information at hand, and the fact that feelings change all the fucking time. Feelings are unreliable as fuck.

The point of our personal development would be going from a feeling-based person to a thinking-based one. As a child, we are clueless about the self, and are almost completely feeling-based. So, back then, your wants weren't decided by keeping the 'self' in mind. It was simple. Whatever made you feel good became your wants—whatever you enjoyed, that's what you wanted to do all the time. Well, life was simple back then, and you were pretty fucking stupid.

So, naturally, as an adult that shouldn't be the case, right? You are supposed to have grown into a thinking person now; well, have you? Have your wants changed from what they used to be when you were a kid—simply being happy all the time? What about other people? Are most of them still chasing after whatever makes them feel good and excited, as answers to being happy?

Two reasons why most of us remain feeling-based happiness junkies:

- Nobody tells us this: Life is a lot of things that have nothing to do with happiness, **but** if you do them right, the result is going to be happiness. In short, happiness is a by-product of life done right. And I hope this does not come as a surprise, but doing things right requires thinking, a lot of it.

The more you chase after feeling good, the more your ass is going to be kicked by life because, in doing so, you ignore all those important things you need to do.

The more you focus on thinking, the better the decisions you make keeping in mind not feelings, but long-term, stable results.

- The want to be happy in the moment **works temporarily.** What you are running after is momentary happiness. So, you do experience short bursts of pleasure whenever you are having fun in your teen years and twenties. It works quite well up until you are forced to realise the distinction between momentary and long-term happiness. The realisation comes after **years** of failed attempts to try and stretch those momentary pleasures into long-lasting ones. This could very well be in your thirties. Do you know what this means? That, even as an adult you continue chasing after a definition of happiness and a list of what makes you happy which you came up with when you were a fucking kid.

Why? Because it made that kid happy, you think the same will continue working with an adult too. Well, this goes to show that most people are simply children who have aged.

HOW HAPPINESS SCREWS YOU OVER AND OVER!

Let's now discover the unique ways in which the childish want to be happy continues to fuck people throughout the course of their adult life.

Have you heard people say this:

1. *Why am I not happy even though I have a great life?*

It's because 'the list of what makes you happy' was decided back when you were a clueless, confused kid. And you stuck with that list because it did bring you momentary happiness from being accepted by and having relationships with fantasy people, fantasy experiences, and even achieving some milestones in your career for the approval of these fantasy people. But the focus on the self consistently remained dormant. Therefore, the result now is: you know how to be happy in the moment, but you aren't satisfied because you have a very distant relationship with your 'self'. You are still as clueless about who you are and what makes your 'self' happy as you were fifteen fucking years ago.

As a side note, now you know when philosophers said

Know thyself, it wasn't some simple thing you didn't need to think much about, it meant your fucking life.

2. *I know I shouldn't be with them, yet I can't stop loving them. I can't stop chasing after them. I can't move on from that person.*

You can't because a part of you is genuinely convinced that their union with your existence brings you the ultimate happiness. You feel that way because of the happiness that you once felt with them, which according to your mind is 'the best feeling ever'. And because your goal in life is to be happy, and you currently don't know of any other happiness better than what you felt with them, you obsess over them even though their presence is currently brutalising you with pain. If you miss them, it's because they made you happy once. You miss that particular happiness, not them really. You will disregard their existence the moment you find it with another person. It's because you are a happiness-junkie, that hit of happiness is much more valuable to you than your self-respect, mental health and the overall peacefulness in your life. So you say, *fuck it,* and keep going after that hit.

3. *I know I should be working hard, but I waste my day doing bullshit things on my phone, being lazy and useless. And because of that I am filled with regret.*

You don't work, because whatever you do instead of working makes you happy. It's as simple as that. You being lazy does not mean you are dead in those moments. You are still working towards feeling great, quite actively so, by watching some comedy, drama, commentary, news, animal rescue videos, or whatever it is that you watch. You do work a lot—except it's in the direction of gathering information which is of no use to your real work. So, a correct way to voice your displeasure is, *I was unproductive,* not, *I didn't do anything,* because you did plenty of things, they were all just complete shit in terms of productivity. Things that add betterment to your life aren't about making you happy, they're about hard work. And you consciously choose momentary happiness over the betterment of your life because you are fucking addicted to being happy. In short, *fuck life in the long term so I can be happy in the moment,* is what you do.

4. I can't say 'no' to people. Because of this, people often impose themselves on my wants and feelings and take advantage of my niceness.

You can't say 'no' because you can't afford to make people unhappy. If they are unhappy with you, you are unhappy, and you want to be happy. You may tell others: *I became unhappy because I didn't get to do what I wanted,* but the real story doesn't stop there. What you don't tell them is that the unhappiness vanishes the moment you see others being happy with you, despite the fact that you still didn't get to do what you wanted. People being happy with you gives you so much pleasure that it feels like a much bigger reward than what you would feel if you stood up for yourself and said 'no'. In short, because happiness is your priority, self-respect is ignored. And that is why, even though you complain to people about how unhappy it makes you, you keep repeating it, especially with people you desperately want to make happy. And you may do that at the cost of working overtime, sleeping less than planned, disrupting your own plans entirely, all because it gives you a great burst of pleasure for having 'helped them'.

5. *I am a dumbass because I have no idea what I want to do, and others are doing so much better than me.*

You are unhappy because others are doing better than you, in which case you would be happy if you were doing better than others. At any point, the source of your happiness and unhappiness rests in comparison to others. The act of comparing yourself has its basis in nothing but simple observation. A comparison could be triggered from seeing anything and anybody. It could be as vague as comparing yourself to a celebrity, a person you have met for the first time, or a person you have only heard about from others. From that, you conclude: *They are better than me.* How fucking dumb is that?

It is not a comparison of data as much as it is of your perception of them. It is you drowning in sorrow because you have **assumed** they have something that you don't, and that something would make you **happy**. These assumptions exist only because you have no idea what would make your 'self' happy.

And because you don't know that, the entire focus of your mind is on the outside, instead of looking inward for the answers. You are busy wanting what **others** have, learning what makes **others** happy, copying the lifestyles of **others**, coveting what you don't have, and as a result developing a deep sense of disregard and ungratefulness towards what you do have.

6. *Life was so much fun back then, life was great. I wish we could go back and live like that forever!*

The thing is, you were the happiest at your stupidest self—when you were young, in college, school, with your friends. You were experimenting with rebellion against structure, engaging in activities that produced rewards (like gaming), entertainment (with friends) and pleasure (partying, dating, alcohol, weed, fun). What you don't realise is that, at that time, you could afford that experimentation. There was no real structure. You were free of any responsibilities, duties and consequences. You were in a safe environment. Now, you are not. What worked then won't work now because the rules, environment and your age have changed, but your want to be happy has not. This explains the confusion as to why the same degree of happiness is not reachable anymore; hence, you blame 'growing up' for it.

If 'growing up' was the problem, then you are suggesting a life without responsibilities, duties and consequences is better, and that is called escapism. As a kid, your reality was structurally designed to keep you as free as possible, therefore those wants worked. **That** reality was manipulated, the current one is not. Ask any person whose life growing up was a continuous battle with tragedy, troubles and struggle if they wish to go back, and you will know the difference. Your responsibilities, duties and consequences pose as a problem to you because you are a grown-person with the wants of a clueless kid—to be happy all the time.

All of the above problems revolve around four things:

- Making yourself happy.
- Making others happy to make yourself happy.
- Making yourself sad because others are presumably happy.
- Making yourself sad because you used to be happy.

The common link, as you can see, is seeking happiness. We keep prioritising it because we are convinced that happiness is what we want from life, and that it is the ultimate answer. In doing so, we tend to de-prioritise most things that have nothing to do with happiness. They could be your self-respect, conscience, morality, rational thinking, common sense, logic and self-betterment. I am pretty sure that, right now, you would choose the other things as they sound sensible. But, in life, it is not possible as long as you are convinced that happiness is the final goal. You have to chuck that thought out of your mind. You have to say, *fuck happiness. I don't want to be happy, I want to be **satisfied** in life. I want self-satisfaction.*

How do you make that transition? Let's talk about it in the next chapter.

CHAPTER NINE

CHOOSE SATISFACTION, NOT HAPPINESS

Mind you, self-satisfaction does contain precise knowledge of what would make the 'self' happy, but it's only one part of the whole picture.

Self-satisfaction starts with the **knowledge** of the self. The thing with knowledge of such kind is, when it's not applied, it gets locked up in the theoretical side of your brain to be used later when you wish to sound smart or give smart advice. Knowledge of self, therefore, can only be **achieved** by knowing with certainty that it **works** when applied in reality.

LET'S ANALYSE WHAT MAKES YOU HAPPY

So, what is it that makes you happy currently?

Well, it could range from your phone to your friends to that person you love. It doesn't matter if it is productive or unproductive. We are looking at everything. It could be reading books, listening to podcasts, watching documentaries, and it could be wasting time with friends, getting high, watching endless bullshit videos, and scrolling through pictures of people to jerk off to—whatever you do.

I want you to start looking at whatever you do with an assumption: you would be fine without everything you currently believe makes you happy.

You might wonder: *How is that helpful?*

The thing about whatever you think are your wants is, they probably haven't been chosen by you. You have to understand, to a *lot* of people and companies, you are a customer, you are part of a statistic, you are a target audience. You are being sold new wants every day. Your mind is being fucked with properly so you choose and like certain things. To put it differently, those things are designed in a certain way so that your mind will like them.

You may say: *Well, even if I am manipulated to like something, I still like it. If I didn't, I wouldn't be doing it.*

Fair argument on the outside, but what it lacks is choice. Manipulation tends to seriously fuck with your ability to make a rational choice. Manipulation feeds on weaknesses and vulnerabilities. Anything that is built on targeting your weakness and naivety, and making you its customer, is fucking vile because it doesn't care about you at all. It doesn't care about your age, maturity and personal development either. You are a user—that's all it cares about.

Most of our wants come from:

- Whatever society has made you believe is awesome (conditioning).
- Whatever you see and have learned that others want (following others).
- Whatever appears to be exciting to you (your impulse).

So when you assume, 'I will be fine without everything I currently believe makes me happy', you question the source and legitimacy of what your wants are. Are they even chosen by you? That's the current point.

Whatever your wants are, let's divide them into two categories: the first would be wants that contribute to long-term results; the second would be wants that bring you momentary happiness. Let's call the first category 'value', because they bring value to your life, and let's call the second 'interest', because they deal with your actual interests in life.

LONG-TERM HAPPINESS

Under value or long-term results, your wants are further divided into two sections: stability and cultivation.

Stability: Doing these things give a structure to your future and the opportunity to make it even better. They make you aware of what you want from your day, what you don't want, and what you want only in controlled quantities. Doing them makes you feel glad and gives you purpose in life. They tend not to give instant happiness, but help you get closer to peacefulness.

Cultivation: Doing these things helps in the cultivation of your mind, for example, listening to a podcast which gives you knowledge and different perspectives, watching movies or TV shows that make you think, and watching and listening to people who help you figure out better ways to deal with daily struggles and needless desires.

They give you reference points and clarity about 'self', not just mere viewing pleasure. Do you at times watch particular scenes from movies because they instantly make you focused? You do that because they have become reference points and reminders to what your self wants. Therefore, whenever you're unmotivated, they help bring clarity instantaneously.

Any of your wants that serve stability and cultivation majorly influence how you think in life, the choices you make and how you see things.

So, out of all your actions and activities that you may call your daily wants, how many fall under 'value'? Your first answer may be: *Absolutely nothing.*

Don't worry, it's very common. People usually prepare themselves when there is an urgency and need. Without those, we tend to just keep doing whatever we do normally.

People tend to realise the importance of the category 'value' when they look back on their lives and say, *You know, I could have done this. I know I could have. I had what it takes in me, but I wasted my time doing stupid shit.*

The realisation comes late, usually when you believe that the opportunity or time has passed. By opportunity, it could be anything—a skill, personality development, or developing control over certain tendencies in you that have led to harm in your career and relationships. It's one of the worst feelings, knowing you could have controlled and changed the outcome of something that now you regret: *If only I had realised it at the right time.* There is no known deadline for the 'right time', only the truth that it will come. The only sensible thing you can do to protect what matters is **prepare** yourself for it. That's how you prosper in the long run, by thinking, knowing and acting on what's best for the long run—financially, mentally, sexually and physically.

Your second answer could be: *I am doing nothing that would fall under stability, but I do read, watch, and learn from things that would come under cultivation.*

That's great, that you invest in the cultivation of your mind. This means that you have come in contact with something that not only made sense to you but took you to a place where you were alone and thinking.

But here's a problem, at times, when people find something that makes them think as an individual, they don't hold on to it, instead they do something that ruins this particular experience entirely for them.

This is what they do: you found something that made you think, but then you shared it with the person closest to you, **expecting** them to either feel the same thing you did, or start thinking that way, or be impressed by you for sharing it.

When they don't express the same excitement, chances are you put the whole thing behind you. *I guess they didn't like it.* Basically, they spoiled it for you.

When they don't agree with the idea, you might see the idea as a failure because it didn't work on them.

When they are impressed by you, you feel kind of smart for having sent them content that they thought was clever and deep—and that's where your focus stays. In all three cases, the idea is not further discussed, debated or developed in your mind; instead, it is forgotten in a matter of days. Always remember: the true test of any idea is not its popularity, but how deeply it makes *you* think.

From now on, any time you feel anything is making you think, it's an **indication** that you need to look into it more. Don't move on. Do not care about the responses of others if you share it with them. It speaks to **you**; therefore, develop it further in your mind. It could be about anything—religion, relationships, social work, dating, or human behaviour. You need to test the idea by imagining if this was a strict want or rule in your life, does it make you more in control and more secure, or not? This could lead you to discover an actual want of yours.

The point of cultivation is not storing knowledge in your mind so you can use it later to impress people. That might make you knowledgeable, not intelligent. It's pointless if it doesn't reflect in your actions. Cultivation of the mind means keeping what makes you think and applying what makes sense.

So, you need to ask yourself right now, how many daily wants and actions of yours are geared toward serving stability and cultivation? If 'not many' or 'none' is your answer, it's a serious concern, my friend. Sooner or later, you will have to take hold of the steering wheel of your life, you might as well start thinking about it now.

Let's talk about the second category.

SHORT-TERM PLEASURES

The second category, called 'interest', would be further divided into two sections: experiential joys and intellectual joys.

Experiential joy: Doing these things gives you a genuine sense of joy that **separates** you from the world or makes you forget the world, for example, riding a bicycle, lifting weights, running, writing, playing an instrument, dancing, spending time with a certain friend, cooking, reading about a subject or creating something. There's a deep connection you have with these activities, and you possessively call them **'yours'**, therefore, these are wants spawning from your 'self'.

So, out of all your actions and activities that you may call your daily wants, how many fall under experiential joys?

You may say: *I can think of many things that give me immense joy.*

Do these give you a sense of thrill, excitement, a rush of happiness? Of course. Do these also give you satisfaction, a personal connection and a freedom of sorts? Those are the ones that would come under 'interest'.

There are a lot of things you do on a daily basis that are either done out of habit or an addiction to the short bursts of pleasure. They may not necessarily be requested by your self. They are done because, if you thought about your current state of affairs, you'd be pretty bummed out—they serve as an escape. They are activities you do to squeeze out some happiness because you wanna run away from facing the truth. So, watching videos endlessly, gaming out of a crippling need to secure a rush of excitement, hanging around with your friends out of habit, or desperately texting random people to get some sex may seem like they fall under experiential joys, but in reality it's just you unable to deal with your shit, and therefore finding a person to solve it for you, or an activity to make you forget about it.

Your wants and actions come under the category 'interest' only when they are controlled **by you**, not you **by them**. Only then can they be comparable to things like working out, riding a bike, cooking, playing an instrument, most of which are highly controlled activities. The thing to remember is: they don't tend to take over you.

So, from today, start noticing what activities and wants of yours are controlled by you, and give you satisfaction in doing them, not just a short burst of pleasure; the activities you feel positively possessive and sure about. And screw those activities you do to escape from the duties and responsibilities of your life—they are gonna fuck you over in the long run.

Let's move on to intellectual joys.

Intellectual joy: Doing these things stimulates your mind, thereby captivating your interest, for example: solving somebody's problem, having intellectual discussions, collecting information about people's lives and using them at opportune moments—no need to be embarrassed in admitting that to yourself—learning and reading about whatever it is that draws your curiosity and interest.

Ask yourself what stimulates your mind and captures your interest. Those would be your real interests. So, out of all your actions and wants, how many fall under intellectual joys?

Your answer could be: *I can think of some activities that definitely capture my interest, but I have never thought of putting time in them.*

Well, it's because time is limited, and your time is already divided between shit you do to fit in this weird world and stuff you have to do in life, such as school or a job. You have a limited number of hours in a day that you can spend on only a certain number of activities. Therefore, you are presented with a choice: either do what everybody around you is doing, or focus on what interests you.

Focusing on what interests you may separate you from others as that choice deviates from the things that people around you are generally doing. This would mean isolating yourself from time to time, risking losing your position in your friend circle, becoming a 'weirdo' in the eyes of others because *you are always doing your thing,* and saying no to activities that people want you to do with them.

So, we have a problem: on one hand, you want to belong, you want to be a part of something, you want to be accepted; on the other, choosing what interests you requires you to say *fuck that* to all of the above. That's what individuality is—breaking out of the group identity and becoming your own person.

So, what is it that you want? Do you want to be an individual or a fucking follower? If you choose individual, then start investing in whatever draws the attention and interest of your self. That is your thing, dude. Investing in it and growing it is what separates you from everybody—that is what makes you an individual, because you are doing your own thing. Put whatever you find intellectually stimulating above what everybody else is doing. Fuck them and fuck that.

And while we are at it, let's look at this group bullshit too.

WOULD COOL FRIENDS MAKE YOU HAPPY?

What do people do in groups? Who decides what is to be done? Is it really democratic or some moron making all the decisions? Are your interests and betterment considered or is it just focused on having fun? Do these people even know what the fuck they are talking about, or are they making shit up as it goes?

Whatever groups you are a part of, think about it.

Most of the stuff you do with people is done for two reasons:

- To be **liked by people.** A lot of activities that you do may not necessarily give you great joy. You may not even understand why people do them, but you don't say no because their mass appeal is too strong. In certain cases, you don't even entertain saying no. There is a chance that you might have convinced yourself that something is wrong with you for not

understanding the appeal of it, so you force yourself
to do that thing.

- To **stay in a group.** This group may have nothing to
  do with like-mindedness, sensibility, boundaries or
  goals and exist simply to fulfil the purpose of having
  fun. Your fear is that if you stayed out of this group
  for a while, you might lose out on fun-filled activities,
  fall behind on whatever the group is 'thinking', and
  will be replaced.

At the end, it's about acceptance. You don't want to be
lonely and discarded, so you are willing to do any stupid
shit—regardless of whether or not it makes sense to you,
whether or not you want to do it—because you think
being in a group and having a lot of friends is a great
statement about you. You are accepted, hence you are of
value. Isn't that herd-thinking?!

That is why, even if you are not in a group, you are
still doing the same things that everybody around you is
doing—to fit in. You are super scared of being a loner. You
have the wants and fantasies of having cool friends and
cool experiences. You are reading and watching videos on
how to be awesome, impressive and an extrovert. *How do
I stop being shy?* Because that will change everything, right?
Once that is out of the way and you have the approval of
people, everything will be great, right? That's some epic-
level bullshit.

People go away, they don't give a shit about you, people give a shit about themselves; so you better start giving a shit about yourself the right way. Time passes, people leave, and you are the one who stays with yourself. Therefore, people are not the answer, it is you who has to find the answers from within you.

So, in case you are called weirdo, strange, nerd, geek, crazy, loner, were unpopular while growing up **because** you **chose** to do what wasn't regarded as popular, chose against mindlessly participating in general happiness, gave attention and time to what interested you and stimulated your mind, then you are on the right path.

Lastly, as far as friendship is concerned, a single person who truly gives a shit about you can replace thousands who claim friendship. So, you know whom to keep.

KNOWING YOURSELF IS A SUPERPOWER

In your answers to what wants of yours came under 'value' and 'interest', there might have been confusion in your mind regarding their placement. You're not supposed to get it right away. It takes time. But at least the process of thinking has begun, which is much better than being a blind follower. Thinking gets you closer to knowing, which is a superpower. Knowing yourself is single-handedly the greatest superpower any person can have. So, try to know thyself as much as you can.

CHAPTER TEN

SCREW PLEASING PEOPLE

DOES YOUR SELF-WORTH COME FROM SELF?

Let's talk about self-worth. What does it mean? It means that you are valuable. How do we get this? It is self-worth after all; the first thing it requires is a 'self'. When you have a self to serve, the self tells you what the worth is. When you don't, you have to depend on others. When they give you confirmation of having worth, you feel happiness. Let me repeat that once again: you depend on others to tell you what your worth is, and this arrangement makes you happy. Out-fucking-standing, mate.

Let's see in how many ways it is done:

1. *By seeking the approval and acceptance of people who are capable and awesome in your eyes.*

You know who they are. *He told me I am capable, doing great, and deserve to be on top. It makes me feel great and more motivated than ever.*

Side note: we are gonna be talking about this at great length in the coming chapters. For now, let's just leave it here and move on to the next thing.

THOSE WHO FEEL SUPERIOR TO OTHERS

2. *By assuming a sense of superiority.*

Think about people you've met who gave you this vibe: *I have a lot of knowledge about things. I love learning about interesting things. I watch clever, obscure movies only meant for intelligent people. I like to watch lectures and documentaries on subjects. My views are really interesting and unique. I have a highly developed taste in movies, art, and music.* You get the idea.

All of this is actually fine until the motive of expressing the above becomes: *I am better than normal people because I am very interesting*—basically accumulating self-worth from assuming you are superior to others.

This involves **showing off** whatever you think is impressive about yourself to others as a **need.** Without it, you won't feel good about yourself. Therefore, it becomes a habit. This is not seeking encouragement, not looking for constructive criticism, nor having a dialogue—actually, far from it. This is a pure display of superiority meant to satisfy the ego.

This is the case of a person whose entire identity is whatever people generally find interesting, so naturally he/

she becomes someone who is knowledgeable, interested in arts and politics, has achievements, and has an opinion on just about anything popular. Yes, this is our self-proclaimed modern-day intellectual. This poor person has no relationship with his or her self; their attention is wholly dedicated to how people see them.

Instead of focusing on the **self** and asking, *what am I interested in, what matters to me, what doesn't interest me regardless of how popular it may be,* their self-worth comes from feeling significant and interesting in the eyes of others. In short, they are dependent on an audience to feel good about themselves.

It's basically being liked on a whole different level. For example, they will refuse to watch or consume something that is widely popular and liked in pop culture by almost everybody. They do this because, if they joined in too, then they would be like everybody else, hence not interesting. Their dismissal might have nothing to do with their actual taste, past choices and true feelings towards that thing. These dismissals simply give them the opportunity to be a contrarian for the sake of being different. That's how desperate they are to be interesting.

Other examples of this would be people saying, *music nowadays is complete shit,* even though they have no knowledge of music or what they actually like. Just because they heard some 'cool' person they follow or older people say that modern music sucks, they do too.

They might even say, *I love listening to Beethoven, Mozart, Bach, you know, real music*, even though, whenever they are alone, they never do, except on occasions in which they have forced themselves to listen to it so they can like it.

Then there are also those who say: *I love watching old movies, especially the ones in black and white, they are classics.* They might have a collection of these movies, which they love to show to people, but actually they haven't watched half of them, and cringe at the idea of re-watching those they have.

There are plenty of people like these; it wouldn't be a surprise if you have met some. Such behaviour exists only because you care about how people see you more than who you are, despite the impression it creates.

Now, it is normal to expect people to like you, but to rely on people to determine your self-worth comes at great risk. What if one day you meet someone who is not impressed? What lengths will you go to impress them, because it's the only way for you to feel you are worthy? What happens the day you meet a person more knowledgeable than you? Does your worth become zero in front of them?

Your depending on others to make you feel worthy carries the equal risk of others making you feel unworthy. Why don't you give all that power to yourself?

Here's the third way we give this power to others:

THOSE WHO COMPARE THEMSELVES TO OTHERS

3. By comparing yourself to people, and winning.

Before we get into this, why do we compare ourselves to others? And more importantly, when do we do this the most?

We compare ourselves because we want to be better than them. And we do this the most when we want to be better than them in the eyes of someone. So, in this case, your self-worth comes from people in the eyes of whom you want to be amazing. These people are the ones with the power, and their approval and appreciation is what gives you self-worth. So, what happens the day you have to work with someone better than you, or someone who has the potential to become better?

You put a target on their back and start competing with them. This, more often than not, is a different type of competition. You are competing with their potential to steal attention and approval, which you believe only you deserve and desperately need. Therefore, such competitions tend to become personal, ugly and filled with animosity.

Ideally, competitions are about proving your capabilities, and losing should culminate in self-reflection. But in these cases, you want to be better than them at any cost. To achieve this, you go beyond their capabilities, you start **comparing** yourself to them with regard to their personal life, the way they talk, the way they behave, their weight, height, looks, their partner, their dress sense and anything else you find worth establishing a superiority in. You talk badly about them and make fun of them to your friends, not realising they now occupy a major portion of your daily thoughts. In your mind, they have become your **nemesis**.

Now, remember: you are doing all of this because deep down you are threatened that they might take away the source from which you feel worthy. All you need to do is, shift that source. You don't need to rely on others to tell you whether you are worthy or not. Are you an adult? Are you capable or not? Fucking decide on your own what standards you want to meet in life, and that's it. Once that's done, you decide what your worth is based on those standards. At least they are coming from your own mind.

Instead, you are busy cock-fighting with this person you have no beef with. It's fucking pointless for three simple reasons: they have nothing to do with you; they don't impact your success at all, only your actions do; and lastly, most of the ways in which you think they are better are based on assumptions.

The only real data you have is work-related. They may be better than you at specific things. But these are also the things you can improve on if you really wanted to.

Here's the honest truth: based on some details you know about them, you may think: *I know this person.* Well, fuck off with that because, in reality, you don't.

You just assume things, and you have to because you are thinking about it so much.

You have no real data on where they come from, what their real-life situation is, what their opportunities were, and how they have managed to make it so far—all of these could easily be far better than you or far worse.

Before dragging yourself down or someone else down, always remind yourself they haven't lived a day in your shoes, and you haven't in theirs. This is happening only because you are triggered from knowing they are better than you in some particular aspect. And it fucks with you because your self-worth comes from the approval of others—that's the source of your problem, not this person.

You know what, let's talk about the source of your problem as well.

DO YOU CARE WHAT OTHERS THINK ABOUT YOU?

Let's think about this: You care so much about what others think about you because you are working under the assumption that people care about you just as much as you do. Well, my friend, welcome to reality—they don't. You are competing with people who are more personable, have better social skills, are more attractive, because you are scared they are going to be better liked **by others** than you. You are ruining your mood over this.

Here's the truth: nobody cares. Nobody cares unless they have a personal motive to care. You have rarely looked at how things are from the point of view of others. If you did, you'd realise that the people you want to impress can barely afford to think about you.

It is just like how you don't have a moment to spare for those who want to be liked by you. You haven't even thought of that, have you? *There are people who want to be liked by me?* There always are, but you rarely pay attention to them because their approval means shit to your self-worth, as opposed to the approval of those who are awesome in your eyes. The same applies to them; at the end of the day, they don't give a shit about you.

People are most interested in their own lives. That does not mean they don't notice people around them. Well, they are interested in people around them because a lot of entertainment comes from people. It's called gossip. And we are social animals. But time and time again, never forget, people are most interested in their own shit. They are busy with their own shit. And they are constantly thinking about their own shit. You place very, very, very low in the list of important things to them, unless you are their partner—personally or professionally—or they have a strong personal motive.

However, important and powerful people do have the ower of offering opportunities, which must be something them. Here's a simple rule: fuck whatever gossip goes around in their mind regarding you. Gossip gets discarded and replaced every day. Lasting impressions are formed by things they cannot ignore. So, impress with abilities, not appearance. Abilities cannot be ignored; if one person happens to do so, there are always going to be other takers.

You have to understand, people may not care about you, but they do make observations. And their approval is nothing more than one of those many observations. They are not just sitting and thinking about you, but that observation does sit at the back of their head, with chances of making a connection with an opportunity. And opportunities as a reward are much better than appreciation.

Appreciation gives you momentary pleasure. Opportunities get you somewhere in life. So apply common sense and tell me, which is better? Doing anything to grab pointless attention or something that benefits you in life?

Try to understand this: the day you can look at a bunch of people all competing with one another to be better in the eyes of someone, and choose to not be a part of that game, is the day you win in the mental battle of life. Look at that figure that you want to impress and see a person in them, nothing but a person just like other people you know. If they have the power to give you opportunities, then focus on what makes one capable get that opportunity. Screw serving that person.

But if you focus majorly on getting appreciation and approval from them, then you are going to focus on who else they appreciate, and then probably compete with them. You will risk ruining your mood on days you performed well but didn't receive their appreciation, and be more inclined to become their followers, their puppets and pawns to their schemes.

You are accumulating self-worth from the appreciation of **others**. That is the root of your problem. Not people who are better than you.

DO YOU RELY ON PEOPLE FOR MOTIVATION?

This is an example of a situation in which you meet awesome people, and are motivated because you realise that you lack self-worth.

Think of the time you attended an event, seminar or conference related to your work or studies. There you met and talked to people who are experts in the field, who have superior skills and more success than you. It gave you immense exposure. While you were there, you felt and thought:

- I am going to be great in this too.
- Why wasn't I working hard all this while? If I were, I would have been impressive too.

Upon returning, you start planning as you experience a surge of inspiration growing in you, and you think about the things you have been wasting your time on. You start cursing, criticising and blaming them. You decide in the moment that you are going to be making changes now and become serious towards work.

And in about ten days or so, you go back to doing what you were doing previously. The new-found motivation is gone. Do you know why that is?

Well, at that event, three things happened:

- In that room, you saw versions of what you can become in terms of success and skills.
- Your self-worth took a severe beating as you weren't the impressive somebody people wanted to talk to or talk about. You were an unknown who talked to impressive somebodies.
- You met with several people who are competent and awesome in everybody's eyes in that room. Therefore, naturally, you wanted to be approved and accepted by them. *One day they're gonna know.*

Hence, the motivation was created by a) wanting success for yourself b) wanting success so you can show to others that you are worthy and c) wanting approval and acceptance of the successful people you met.

Two-thirds of your fucking motivation came from the **outside**, only one-third from inside. When these others left your mind in ten days or so, so did two-thirds of your motivation, and you went back to doing the same things

And then you are sitting with your phone in your hand, wondering why you are not motivated anymore.

As a result, you start glorifying these events in your mind, romanticising the people you met as though they were perfect beings, and blaming more strongly the people in your life as if they have tied your hands. *It's because of them I don't work hard.*

Your problem is your motivation comes from the **outside**, and you have labelled **outsiders** as the ideal source for your motivation. If you want to be crazily motivated to do anything, a hundred per cent of the reasons to do that thing will have to come from the inside. Words like 'others' and 'them' will have to be replaced by 'myself'. It should not be *I wanna show them*, but *I wanna show **myself**,* not *I want to be great so they will be impressed*, but *I want to be great so I can be satisfied with myself.* You have to keep this word in mind: myself. That's who you are; that's the one who gets affected; and that's the one whose life it is.

If you are relying on others, you are indirectly controlled by others. And others don't give a shit about you.

Now, how do we achieve this? Buckle up, my friend, we're gonna take the word 'myself' up a few notches and create a new foundational principle: You are a nation. That's how you will have to start seeing yourself from now on. You are a nation in yourself, and I am going to prove it to you.

CHAPTER ELEVEN

YOU ARE A NATION

BECOMING INDEPENDENT

Before we move on to the nation part, let's make sure we know what our objective is. It is the simple question: how do you extract self-worth, approval, acceptance from your 'self'?

To do this, there needs to be a 'self' first. This means you will have to get to know your self. When you are getting to know your self, you will find out that you have specific wants, desires and tendencies in you. Out of those, you're gonna find out that there are certain things in you which are the enemy. It could be certain desires, some urges in you, or some tendencies which cause self-harm. Basically, they are set out to ruin whatever you wanna build.

When you find out all these things, you realise you need to bottle them the fuck up. You need to control this shit. Therefore, you create self-control. Sounds awesome, right? It is. Self-control creates rules, establishes some morality according to which your actions and choices are going to be regulated from now on. This means you are becoming your own person, as you are taking control of yourself. You have rules now. You have moral grounds which you don't breach.

Now, think about what just happened. The moment you say you have rules and moral codes, you are kinda becoming your own authority. This basically means: for the first time in your life, your self is in charge of you. And when you are able to pull this off for some time, when you are making decisions in your life taking into account what the rules and moral codes are, you experience self-respect. Dayum, this shit is coming together. Self-respect in turn makes you feel that life right now is all right. It makes you feel proud of yourself for making decisions that you want to make. Lastly, self-respect assures you that the 'self' as the current authority is the best for you.

And that, my friend, is the entire game—you being in full control of your actions and decisions. Now, stay with me. What do you think happens when you don't have self-control? Those very tendencies, desires, and urges that are the enemy easily take over you and become the authority. It could be greed, lust, anything. And we see this happen all around us. For example: porn addiction, or some sexual practice that can damage your healthy relationship, or a power-trip that doesn't care about consequences. These are common examples of desires and tendencies that were supposed to be spanked by self-control and kept in check. And that is why self-control is paramount for the self to remain the authority of you. Without it, these fucking enemies can take over and destroy your mental peace.

But it's not only self-control, self-respect is equally important. While self-control takes care of inner demons, self-respect takes care of enemies outside.

Without self-respect, you leave yourself open for people to take over and become your authority. You don't want examples for this, you have seen this shit happen all around you: people doing anything to make someone happy, disregarding their self, their own wants, plans, everything. And not just for love, this happens all over the world for approval, acceptance and self-worth. Yikes. So, self-respect ensures nobody fucks with your authority over your own mind, feelings and wants.

BECOMING A NATION

This is how you need to start seeing yourself from now on:

- You are a nation, not just a person.
- Other people are other nations.
- Your parents, siblings and those you love are neighbouring nations. If you have a good relationship with them, it's great; if not, you both suffer.
- Your 'self' is the president of the nation.

- Your moral code and rules become your constitution. These rules come from knowing what causes harm to the nation. And the moral code ensures what lines you will never cross.
- Self-control is the security force that enforces the rules and moral codes in the constitution.
- Self-respect is the happiness index of your nation. This is felt when self-control does its job well.
- The desire, urges or tendencies in you that cause harm are the terrorists.
- Your ego is the opposition party. It wants you to be the best, but it doesn't know what 'best' is, except that it is a word that makes you feel great. And because of this, the self must govern the ego and work together on certain projects.
- Self-satisfaction is enjoying the prosperity from the results.

Therefore, the foreign policy should be never to give anyone else the authority of your nation. Whether it is desires or people; whether it is for love, approval and self-worth or pleasures; your self should be the authority.

BECOMING DIPLOMATIC

Your foreign policy is as strong as your diplomacy. You're going to meet a lot of people in life. You can't just allow anybody to start fucking with your feelings, which happens a lot. It happens in the name of wanting someone's approval, in the name of being liked by colleagues, and in the name of love.

Why does it happen? The answer is because of that really dumb thing called ego. Your ego cares too much about how people see you, what people think of you, and how to control those two. Well, the honest truth is—you can't, you can't control how people see you and what they think of you. You can watch a thousand videos on how to make people like you, even then you will find some who won't for no specific reasons. And their talking smack behind your back will bother you a lot. The same goes for rejections. People will reject you, and your brain will go: *How dare you reject the awesome creation that is me!*

People are gonna do whatever the fuck they want. You get to control what *you* do and how *you* think—that's your only privilege. So, for your own benefit, in order to shut your ego down, you will have to learn to **let go**. The more you master it, the less you're going to give a fuck about what people think of you.

Letting go can be boiled down to two simple things:

- You can't please everyone.
- You can't control anyone.

Simple enough, right? If you can practise these simple enough sayings in real life, your ego will be in check. You really can't waste your time and go around blaming people for being assholes, because people are none of your business. You have to understand what your ego is doing.

Your ego creates a much higher opinion of yourself than what is true in reality. When you think very highly of yourself, you may have trouble seeing the simple truth. That happens because your head is very far up your ass.

The ego gives you two simple formulas: *I can* and *They can't*.

Here's an example of *I can*. Let's take people who think they are the hottest shit on the planet; therefore, they believe, *I can charm and control any person I want*.

The truth is, soon enough, some person is going to walk into your life and rip apart your plans and strategies to pieces. It will happen because of probability.

And when it happens, your ego is going to be shattered, which might make you obsess over this person. You will do so because your ego doesn't only teach you *I can*, but also: *They can't*.

So, you will see a person unable to be controlled by you, and think: *How dare they do this? How dare they break the pattern of everybody liking me? They can't do this.*

To this, the ego will respond again with more overconfidence—*I can still get them to like me. I will change myself. I will try a new strategy.*

And from then on begins a continuous cycle of *I can control them* and *They can't do that*, in short, *I can* and *They can't*.

God knows how many people have destroyed several years of their lives being stuck in this bullshit; how many people have entered terrible relationships because of this; how many people are doing anything to please someone at the workplace or school. If you too are stuck in this cycle, let them go. It's your stupid ego that has gotten you into this. You are fine.

This cycle prevents you from seeing the reality that is right in front of you. If you cared to look at the reality, the facts would be laid out pretty neatly. But your dumb ego keeps pushing you to focus on how this makes you **feel** instead of what this **means**. This prolongs the suffering and makes you keep going back to them or keep longing for their approval.

The truth is, you can't and they can—and this is where we started. You can't please everybody. You can't control anybody. What you do control is yourself, so why not put all of your focus there? You are a nation, after all.

YOUR EGO IS A DUMB BELIEVER

People, and that includes you, are most interested in themselves. And it is that self-interest which is making you want to be interesting and important in the eyes of people too.

People come and go. How many of them are you going to keep pleasing? And for how long is this strategy going to last? Finally, if they are most interested in themselves, what would make them give a shit about you as much as they give a shit about themselves? You're just a person they know.

Whenever you feel bad or hurt because somebody is acting a little strange, scream that in your mind if you have to: it is your stupid ego getting hurt. You, my friend, are fine. Your reality is exactly how it was. And in reality, it doesn't fucking matter. You can't control people, and you shouldn't have to think about it too. You wanna feel better? Apply the concept of specialness that we talked about in the second chapter. You earn your self-worth. People shouldn't be giving it to you in the first place. You allowed it, so stop it now. You have to become your own complete person, a complete nation in yourself that can take care of itself and is unaffected by other people's bullshit.

So, the question becomes: how do you free yourself? And from whom specifically do you have to free yourself? This, again, will be a journey. We will have to clear a lot of concepts that you have taken for granted, such as heroes, 'good' and 'bad', and about people. Without clarity, change is plagued by confusion. And when you are confused, any person can easily become your authority and make you their follower. All they have to do is convince you that they know more, hence they should direct you. This is a journey on which it will become clear to you that you are capable of directing yourself.

CHAPTER TWELVE

SCREW YOUR HEROES

WHO ARE THESE HEROES?

Think of the individuals whose approval means everything to you. These are celebrated beings who occupy a place of unquestioned authority in your mind. These are the individuals you do not want to disappoint. You get excited when you see them; their every word is wisdom to you; their actions are the right actions; and their achievements and knowledge are what makes you follow them.

In all likelihood, you want to be them. They are basically perfect humans in your eyes.

This is a figure of authority—could be a professor, head of department, mentor or some high achiever you know personally. You get the idea.

You observe how they talk, how they walk, their hand movements, little gestures; and how they conduct themselves in different situations. You are always pretty amazed by whatever the fuck they do, so much so that you try to bring what you learn from them into your behaviour. Your theory is: *However they act must be the right thing to do*. After all, they are perfect beings.

Soon enough, their views become your views, their favourite order in a restaurant is the thing you prefer too, their slang is the ones you use too, their dress sense becomes the right way or the cool way to dress up. Think about it, when you're impressed by someone, you try to copy them; now imagine when you are impressed by someone so much that you think there's nobody better than them. You give them complete authority of yourself. You become their follower.

In this process, there are strong chances that their way of seeing life becomes yours too. The problem is that this doesn't change even when you find something about them that may bother you. It happens because your faith in following them is so strong that you convince yourself of this: *That's how winners think* or *That's what winners do*.

Well, these are the first type of people you need to detach yourself from in your mind if you want to be your own person.

WHY DO WE LOVE HEROES?

If I asked you to say, fuck your heroes; fuck whomever you think is your role model. Would it make sense to you, even if it is necessary for your personal growth?

Even if it doesn't mean that *They are dead to me, I don't respect them, all their ideas are bullshit, all their knowledge is bullshit.* Even if it only meant: Fuck their authority and nothing else; to you, it may seem as a very offensive idea. It would be offensive because, somewhere along the line, you were taught two very powerful words—'heroes' and 'role-models', which meant people who are above normal humans. And when you called somebody that word, they became untouchable and awesome to you.

It happened because that word is absolute; there is no debate about the meaning of this word. And that is how your mind is manipulated by language. You probably would have had strong doubts about who they are as a person until the title 'hero' was assigned to them by you or by society. That word answered who they are as a person—they are a hero or a role-model. Does that actually answer that question? Fuck no. But this word has that power. And that's why you'd be offended, not because it is about that particular person, but because it's about somebody you think is your hero.

Such a simple word, right? Well, that's how you manipulate people—through the simplest of things. No wonder humans are generations of cattle led by wolves.

So, we need to first understand how we bought into this bullshit idea of heroes in the first place.

FROM WHERE DID WE BUY THE IDEA OF HEROES

In general, you have a tendency to mindlessly believe that there are heroes in this world; you see people who do good things as 'heroes'.

And personally, you call people your heroes if you think they are capable and awesome.

This infection in our thought process has been spread from movies, TV shows and the dramatic retelling of historical accounts of people with heroic perspectives. Even though you know the idea of a 'hero' comes from fiction, what you fail to acknowledge is that it ends with fiction as well. We love to bring it into reality.

The truth is, the idea of a hero and villain is very interesting and too damn simple. Even a four-year-old gets it and is gripped by it. A highly intelligent person once wrote, 'Truth is rarely pure and never simple'. This idea is both.

One would think that as we grow older and mature, we would outgrow such simple ideas, but apparently most of us don't. So, this idea develops further into the monochromatic **perception** of 'good' and 'bad'. And without a hint of scepticism, we consider all manner of things from this stupid point of view, such as:

- Political issues: *They are the bad guys, we are the good guys, vote for us because we will keep you safe from the bad guys.*

- Personal opinions on people you meet: *He looks like a good guy.* It is actually the foundation of our first impressions—somebody is either good or bad.

- Your perception of structures of power, fame and money: *The government is bad. Scientists are good. People who work on Wall Street are bad. Teachers are good. Famous actors are good because they play nice people in movies and TV shows and because they support causes.*

When asked about heroes and role-models, our answers always concern themselves with the image of being 'good', without realising that an image can be created—it doesn't necessarily have to be true.

The problem with 'good' and 'bad' is it blinds you to the aspects of being human. People are many, many things, but never wholly good or entirely bad. That would be just like the characters we saw in movies as children.

But we still believe in that and function on that basis because:

- It is a popular idea. So the logic is: everybody thinks like that so it must be right.

- You learned as a child that people who are good cannot be bad, and bad people cannot be good. Sadly, as a grown-up, it still continues to make sense to you.

- You still think like that because you are never taught how to think, question and investigate.

A SOCIETY THAT FUNCTIONS ON 'GOOD AND BAD' IS DUMB

What happens when we continue with the childish perspective of seeing people as either good or bad? The consequences are:

- Because we are self-important beings, we presume that we are ourselves good. Since we all presume that we are good, the only acceptable qualification in public discourse, behaviour and ideology becomes **'being good'**. When we do that, we unknowingly become a mob which judges anything that doesn't look good, doesn't feel good or 'seems' anything but good. So we start judging appearances that we don't like, things that hurt our feelings or things that feel bad. If you think we live in an outrage culture, this is one of its causes. Everything is viewed from the lenses of either good or bad. The nuances are lost. The deeper meanings are lost. The story from both sides is lost. Just feeling bad is enough for people to start judging. Also, we force ourselves and others into corners of privacy to do things that aren't considered 'good' in the eyes of the public. Lastly, we become susceptible to being manipulated by clever people who can easily pose as 'good'.

- We label people as our heroes and role models **without** any scepticism, scrutiny or real data. All they have to do is **sell** us the image of being good successfully and consistently. This happens on television almost every day, through movies, and happens an insane amount on social media platforms.

- The perception of being good is used to build public perception by brands, people, politicians, leaders to gather a following, profit and power for themselves.

- We even label people **around** us as heroes and role models even though it is based on limited interactions and we have no real data about them. The thing that tends to win them such titles in your mind is impressive achievements, which you have been programmed to worship. And just like that, you become a follower and they are your heroes.

A PERSON WHO FUNCTIONS ON GOOD AND BAD IS DUMB

One of the worst things you can do to your 'self' is call someone your hero or role model. The moment you do, they fit into your childish fantasy of being wholly perfect. They stop being people but become something bigger in your eyes. This is dangerous because that's exactly what they are—people.

The concept of good and bad also prevents you from fully empowering yourself and fully accepting others. How do you fully empower yourself?

You do that by finding out and recognising your virtues, as well as tendencies that can do harm to you and others. Then you employ self-control to beat those tendencies into submission. We have talked about this before.

Self-empowerment begins with accepting that you knowingly and unknowingly can cause great damage to yourself and others in the simplest of ways. You have the power to cause great hurt—it could be to your parents, your friends, partner or yourself. You cannot accept this as long as you believe that you are good. And the great majority of us believe that, including you, my friend, whether you would like to admit it or not. You're the protagonist of your story, why would you not assume you are good!

Because we believe that, we start blaming, rationalising, living in denial as much as we can, very believably so, to escape accountability. And why wouldn't we? Doing bad things means inviting shame, humiliation and judgements from people. Who the fuck wants that? And since you have the mental faculties to bullshit yourself, why wouldn't you use them to blame and justify?

The biggest problem is: We **know** what to expect when doing good. We get to feel positive and find acceptance and love from people.

We have **no** idea what to do when we see ourselves as 'bad'. You have nowhere to go because you were never taught how to process this. You hardly ever consider that you might have done something bad by putting yourself in the other person's shoes.

No, you instantly go on the defensive, because 'you are good', which you have to prove now. And what comes as the first impulse is **deflection**:

I didn't do anything bad, they deserved it. I didn't do anything bad, it's because they stopped treating me the way they used to in the past. I didn't go anything bad, it's how the world works—nature, baby. I didn't do anything bad, they didn't care about me either. I didn't do anything bad, I am only looking out for myself, my people, my nation, it's for the greater good of future generations.

It's because of the clusterfuck explained above that we shut the possibility of discovering our self. Instead, we want to be as fake as possible for the sake of seeming good, to be accepted by others and society. In doing so, we also close the possibility for others to fully open themselves to us. It happens because we become judging assholes whose standards are no less than what society approves.

THERE ARE NO HEROES, ONLY PEOPLE

There are no heroes, no good people, no bad people—these are foolish, oversimplified perceptions. We are fully capable of doing acts of various nature, ranging from ethical to evil in different situations at different times with different risk involvement for different personal motivations. You have to accept that people are flawed beings; we are a mix of selfish tendencies, biological urges, our impulses and ego-driven inclinations. In the words of the mighty philosopher of our age, Mike Tyson, 'We are animals trying to become humans.' It's a gradual struggle—for all of us. If, on the same day, you do one good thing and one bad thing, what does that make you? It makes you human.

When you stop seeing people as either good or bad, you expect everybody to be human. This means you are not shocked at learning that a particular somebody who appeared to be all nice, gentle and kind has done some bad shit to people. You might find out that a man you thought is great and wise is unfaithful to his wife, his ambitions are not noble but fuelled by greed, or that he uses his power to seduce younger women by offering them false hopes and promises—it happens all around the world.

Nor are you shocked at learning that some completely unknown person has been committing acts of kindness quite generously without broadcasting how amazing he/she is. And doing that doesn't make them heroes either.

You start seeing people as people and expect the unexpected from them. Once you develop this healthy scepticism, you become aware of the fact that you live and work amongst **people**—neither wholly good, nor wholly bad. You learn to appreciate acts of charity and kindness without awarding titles of goodness to them. You do so because you recognise the same person might have the tendency to act in ways that may not be acceptable, appropriate, or sensitive to others.

Here is an example: You have a colleague in office who goes out of their way to help you with your work. For this, they have your appreciation and gratitude. The choice now could be:

- To see them as a completely 'good' person, which means they are overall generous and good in your eyes. Now remember, the word 'good' implies they are trustworthy. (Assumption.)
- Or to simply see them as a person who is helping you out, for which you are more than thankful. But your trust in them is limited to the fact that they will help you without expecting anything in return from you, since this has been your experience with them so far. (Data.)

When you see them as someone who is only helping you out, you recognise that you don't fully know them as a person. You recognise they may have ulterior motives and you don't form your opinions about them until further knowledge about them is gained. Meanwhile, what you do have is the choice of rewarding their help in words, with a present or by helping them out when they need it.

Now let's say that they do have ulterior motives, if you thought of them as a good person you can trust, not only will you be shocked, but they can have the power to make you feel guilty for having taken their help. When something like this happens, the only choice left with you is to now see them as a bad person—which is again stupid as fuck. Bad is a strongly negative word in your mind. And if you are sharing your work environment with a person you think is bad, it becomes a negative environment because they are right fucking there.

But if you saw them as a human from the start, you wouldn't be surprised at learning about their motives because, at the back of the head, that possibility always existed. Therefore, you would have prepared yourself for any scenario. You were prepared for any situation in which they made it weird or tried some shady shit with you. That clarity can only come when you remove the perception of bad and good, and start seeing people as people only—all of them. When you think like that, not only are you more aware of what motives people can have, your reasoning is carefully regulating your naive assumptions, and you keep yourself in a position which doesn't give anybody's motives a chance to work on you.

When you stop seeing people as good or bad, you start paying attention to them with respect to what you **want**.

Let's take the example of role models. Say you have met a person who is experienced, an achiever who has the power to help and influence your career. You want their guidance; actually, you want as much help as you can get.

When you realise there are no heroes, only humans, they remain just people in your eyes. The process of idealising them, idolising them, or romanticising them as heroes stops. And with it, you stop granting them the armour of ethics. *They are impressive at what they do, hence they are my heroes, hence they are **good**.* That doesn't make any sense, but we think like this a lot.

When you stop this, they become like every other person. You start seeing them as flawed people instead of perfect beings. Therefore, your focus stays on the relationship between their capabilities and what you can gain from them. You don't become their follower. Your behaviour is guided by expectations of what they can offer with no compromises to your principles, self-control and self-respect. As a result, they don't become the authority in your mind—your **self** retains that position.

Lastly, when you see people as people, you rely on data to find out who they are. You don't care about the impressions they create or how people behave around them. For example, if you find out something you don't like, it is based on **real data** about that person—they have exhibited behaviour you don't want to associate yourself with. The problem with flatly labelling them as 'good' is that you close all the possibilities of them having any ulterior motives for which they might be helping you. When you see them as a person, you recognise you don't fully know them. Therefore, you don't form any opinions until real data on them is gained. To quote Mike Tyson again: Everyone that you fight is not your enemy and everyone who helps you is not your friend.

THERE ARE NO HEROES, ONLY HEROIC ACTIONS

There are no heroes. There are heroic actions though. This expectation of being a hero is projected on people **by you**.

It's an expectation any sane person would rarely choose for themselves. The title of being a hero can very easily ruin a person's life, because it comes with the expectation that all their actions, all their decisions and relationships and every single behaviour in their past and present must be pure and good.

Any instance from their past that reflects the action of a greedy, selfish, ignorant, prejudiced or lustful person— characteristics that **people** are known to have—can not only dismantle their title of hero, but defame them for the rest of their lives. Once you call a person a hero, they are disqualified from being human anymore.

We should admire heroic actions, encourage them and celebrate them; we should aspire towards incorporating them into our lives. But we should leave those people to be people, and to act like people—*that's a great thing they are doing, I really admire it*—and spare the person from your dumb expectations and assumptions regarding things you have no data about.

Hopefully, you will no longer hand over your authority to people because they have the capacity to impress you with power and knowledge. Keep your authority to your own nation.

Now, what about those people who you believe are heroes and saviours of humanity? Let's talk about them as well.

CHAPTER THIRTEEN

ADMIRE, NEVER FOLLOW

WHAT ABOUT THE PERFECT PEOPLE YOU FOLLOW?

Your heroes are people. This means no matter how glamorous, impressive, commanding, rich, celebrated, famous and respected they are, they too have feelings and flaws just like you do.

They too cry, bitch and moan like everybody else. They too struggle to do many things and face disappointments. They too have inner demons. They also wonder: what's the point of everything? And question their achievements. They too have regrets, wish they could have done some things differently, and make mistakes. They are humans after all, aren't they?

They are either imagined as perfect beings by you or are advertised to you as perfect beings by self-promotion, what is written about them and by people who follow them. You know, a lot of these supposedly 'perfect people' have companies and foundations that focus only on recruiting more and more followers. And this is how we create enlightened **perfect** beings. Their perfection could be based on either the stories you have heard about them, the huge number of their following, or the impact their speeches have had on you.

So, how many of these do you follow? Here's the truth: Nobody's perfect.

But, of course, you have heard this before from one of these 'enlightened' beings. And when you heard this, you excluded them from the statement, because if they were like everybody, they wouldn't have told you that nobody's perfect; therefore, it doesn't apply to them, *yaay, I am so smart, I should totally follow them.*

NOBODY'S PERFECT.

But what about those people who seem to have solutions for all your problems? Problems which to them are ordinary, mundane bullshit that only ordinary people have to deal with every day? NOBODY'S PERFECT! Not them either.

All right, but what about our forefathers, freedom fighters, authors, scientists, inventors, philosophers, and great historical figures who paved the way for freedom, equality and justice for future generations? Those who annulled harmful practices, fought ignorance, prejudice and oppression? Are we to believe they were not great, perfect men and women? Are the pioneers of new-age inventions, technology and advancement not worthy of being followed as perfect examples? Even the ones who lead with principles of non-violence and total inclusiveness?

No, none of them was perfect. They were all people with plenty of flaws. And you should never get the idea of following them or anybody, because in the word 'follow' comes the wish of emulating and becoming like them. And you cannot change and become who they are just because you would like to. It doesn't work like that. You will remain who you are, so it's better you get in touch with that and work on it. What you can do is take what you admire about them and try to bring that into your behaviour and thinking as well. You can try that with the help of self-control.

What you should strive for is to be a mix of:

- Who you are, which comes by giving your 'self' the authority.
- And what you admire about them.

Although the need to follow somebody comes from admiration, there is a huge difference between saying: *I admire them* and *I follow them*.

WHAT IT MEANS TO ADMIRE SOMEONE

When you say you admire something about somebody, you point exactly towards what appeals to your mind. Your focus stays on the **source** of your admiration, which could be their actions, beliefs, creativity, or their intelligence.

Admiration could also mean that you take inspiration from that source, which means their work is a point of reference for you, not something you want to copy. You can be inspired by somebody's work and go on to create something of your own. People do that more often than not.

Lastly, when you admire something about somebody, you are free to distance yourself from everything else but those aspects that cause the admiration. You do not have to become their followers.

WHAT IT MEANS TO FOLLOW SOMEONE

When somebody is your hero, you take on the mantle of being their follower. With that mantle now comes the responsibility of proving why they are worthy of being followed and defending them when somebody disagrees with you or attacks them. You might think, *I don't have to defend anybody, it's my choice, I will follow whoever I want.*

That's bullshit. The truth is that your choice to follow them now represents your intelligence. And failing to defend them makes you look like an idiot.

Think of all the people you call your role models. When anybody criticises them, you get all salty and feel the need to defend them. But the moment they pull out some information about them indicating a lack in moral character, these figures become harder to defend. The truth is, you yourself at some point questioned your heroes upon learning certain details about them which were very human-esque and not very hero-like. But because the aura of the hero-figure loomed so large in your head, you chose either complete denial or some cockamamie bullshit explanation to shut down the doubt once and for all.

The same applies to historical figures. They are your heroes for having had a strong impact. But what happens when you learn unsavoury facts about their lives? Perhaps they had multiple affairs with much younger women; perhaps they cheated on their wives; or they plagiarised an idea; or they were prejudiced towards a group of people; or they were violent.

Do any of these facts negate their acts of heroism or unbridled creativity? Do they contradict the idea of a perfect moral hero you learned as a child? What it most certainly does is put a question mark after hero in your mind, because even with your admiration for them still intact, those facts do fuck with you—facts that make them human. And anytime you are discussing their greatness and someone brings them up, you become quiet, your narrative falls apart.

You want to prove they are heroes, when all they are is human, with slightly more conviction in their beliefs and a drive that lead them to commit those great actions.

YOU DON'T HAVE TO FOLLOW ANYBODY

You are a fan of their extraordinary acts and the products of their talents, **not** their lives. Learn to differentiate. What you have is a fascination for their lives. Without their achievements, you wouldn't have even known their names. Why not admire them for those acts alone! If we only looked at the acts objectively, almost everybody would unanimously agree that they are worth admiring. Why not leave it at that? As previously discussed, the entire system of calling people heroes or role models is childish.

Should we subjectively decide based on how much we like them whether the wrongs they did matter to us or not? Or should we compare the impact of their bad decisions to their acts of greatness? Or maybe, it's not our responsibility. It was theirs. It was their life. Your responsibility lies to your life. They never appointed you as their spokesperson to defend them. The only thing you can do is learn from them. You don't have to follow anybody.

Admire whatever it is that appeals to you and aspire to learn and incorporate **that** in your actions by beginning to **try**. You have your own self, which you should build into something you can be proud of and be satisfied with. And to do that, you learn from **everybody**.

There are three facts of life:

- There is no person on this planet with whom you would agree on everything one hundred per cent.
- There is no person on this planet with whom you would disagree on every single thing.
- There is no person on this planet from whom you cannot learn something new.

So, learn from everybody. Maybe that is why we label people as heroes—because we are flawed. We need heroes to believe in our hearts that we can be better, so there is hope for us too. Well, the fact that you want to be better is the hope. But for that, you don't have to be like anybody, you already have your 'self'. There is only one person who should give you approval, acceptance and self-worth, and that is you. You are a nation, my friend. Build a self-reliant one.

CHAPTER FOURTEEN

THE PIECES OF SHIT ONLINE

Now, it is not entirely your fault that you follow people. Two major drivers are assumptions and advertisement. Basically, there are a lot of pieces of shit who leech onto your fascinations, naivety and vulnerabilities and get you to become their followers—a lot of them on the internet right now. Let's broadly look at people that we tend to follow.

In terms of their impact on people, we would have four categories:

- Those with less impact and more entertainment.
- Those with high impact and high entertainment.
- Those with high impact and entertainment and knowledge.
- Those with high impact and perfection.

Now, not all of these are pieces of shit, only a lot of them are—it's important to differentiate.

THE TRUTH ABOUT SOCIAL MEDIA INFLUENCERS

Before we get deeper, let's set a few things straight about the internet and these social media influencers.

- We live in a world where it has always been the norm to gather a following. This means that, throughout history, a few people have always tried to gain a following for themselves for several reasons: to acquire power, wealth, influence, popularity and control. All right?

- People by nature are aspirational beings. Aspirational content means selling you things that you don't have but would like to have. We have these wants as we live under the impression that these things will make us happy. The truth is, we think this way because we have no fucking idea what would make our 'self' happy. So we chase after bullshit ideas of happiness being sold to us by YouTubers and vloggers.

- Since you are shown only what they want you to see, you **assume** it is real. This is where you develop the *why am I not like them* syndrome.

Now, here's the most important point: The element of honesty is what separates blind following and admiration.

The more honest the person you follow is, the less you would feel like emulating them and becoming them. The more dishonest a person is, the more you want to become like them.

Honesty removes the cloak of perfection from your eyes. What you see are normal, approachable people with flaws and struggles, just like yourself. Therefore, you admire them for their realness.

With dishonesty, the narrative of whatever they want to sell you remains in their control. And they sell you perfection—it could be a perfect life, perfect happiness, perfect intelligence or whatever you might dream about having. Since you have no real data about who they really are behind the screen, you **assume** they are perfect from what they show you—which is bullshit.

Therefore, the more honest a person, the more you **admire** them. The less honest a person, the more you **follow** them.

The focus boils down to real data and honesty. Everything else is advertisement and assumption. Now, let's talk about the four types of influencers.

THE INFLUENCERS YOU DON'T GIVE A SHIT ABOUT

1. *Those with less impact and more entertainment.*

You have watched their stuff, you know their names, but don't really give a shit about them. And you would think it remains like that, but it doesn't. You see, these people, once upon a time, were just like you. They too followed a bunch of cool, aspirational influencers and wished they could be like them one day.

Now, when they are able to accrue a large enough following, they believe they are ready to be a part of that group. Therefore, spreading stereotypes of perfection seems exciting to them. To them, it's finally living out their own fantasies and choosing to spread the same lies that they once bought themselves.

Think of any influencer who in the beginning of their career appeared humble, sincere and **relatable** to you. But after fame and money, they became more and more fancy, their pictures became more professional, their flaws started to vanish, their clothes became more expensive, their relationships seemed more for camera and status, and their attitude became more self-absorbed.

You may think it is fame and money that changed them, but the truth is they were this person all along. It's just that, without the fame, they couldn't show it.

Now, not all influencers make this choice. Those who do embrace the persona of celebrities and start selling you unattainable types of perfection.

FAMOUS PEOPLE YOU GIVE A SHIT ABOUT A LOT

2. *Those with high impact and high entertainment.*

These are people about whom you say: *I care about them very much.* Not only do they provide high doses of entertainment, their personal life is of equal importance to you. You are fascinated by them, call them your role models, heroes, and identify yourself as their faithful follower.

You are either in love with a **persona** created by them for you, or a persona you created of them as a follower. *I know who they are because I am their true fan.* You have assumed a thousand things about them, making them fictional characters. The truth is: you don't know shit. You haven't lived with them.

They control the narrative of what is being shown to you at all times. You hardly ever get true stories about them from people around them, or people who have worked with them. When they talk about each other, it's the same script about how great it was working with that person, and how great that fucking person is. It's the same circle-jerk, even though they may privately hate each other.

You have no idea how they really think, what their actual wants are, and how they really behave with that much power. Now, you can get some idea by applying common sense. For example, how do you think people would behave if they got millions of dollars and a lot of fame—basically a pill that gave them insane, unimaginable power? If you can't imagine that, just take the people you know, like your friends; how do you think they would behave? They would lose their fucking minds. I am not saying all of them; maybe 10 per cent won't, but the rest of them, only god knows.

And you think you know these famous people. Here's the thing: if you like them because they are great artists, that's cool. But when you say they are your role-models or heroes without knowing shit about them, that's a tendency of a follower which is making you dumber.

Why can't we be a society that admires somebody's talent or message, and not make assumptions about them because we don't fucking know them at all?

Now, sometimes, these famous people shine a light on mental health issues and causes, which is great. They are powerful people, so their message has a huge audience. Whether they are doing it to build their public image or not, it doesn't matter. It helps the issue.

But when they talk about personal issues, like break-ups or hardships of any type, we lose our minds. If being aspirational didn't have such a ridiculous market value, you would have known they go through exactly the same problems as you do, with the exception of money-related ones. You are surprised because your perception of them is they are perfect beings from outer space.

Now, here's something very interesting: An opposite reaction is created when the same people have private information leaked about them. They get involved in scandals, are found hiding money, cheating on their partners, mistreating people around them, or doing something that shatters that image of perfect beings.

As a result, you get mad at them. *I am so disappointed with them. I never expected this from them.* You feel betrayed, as if you knew them personally. The only thing you knew about them was the bullshit persona they were selling you through movies or YouTube videos. How many times are you going to fall for the same trick?

It reveals the intensity of your emotional involvement in their personal life—about which you know absolutely nothing, but have assumed everything. Why don't you **ignore** the persona they are selling and screw the assumptions your mind is creating, and only **admire** what made you notice them—entertainment, art, intelligence, skills. They are people. Their skill in a few things doesn't preclude them from having flaws, desires, urges, as all people do. Screw the aspirational value, *I wish I could be like them;* they are just people, so are you. Be who you are.

THOSE WORTH GIVING A SHIT ABOUT

3. *Those with high impact and knowledge.*

These are people you love to watch, but don't follow in life. They have won your admiration several times, but don't quite appeal to your aspirational ambitions. They are too real, relatable and rebellious.

Take the example of stand-up comedians. Their status of being aspirational is ruined by their occasional self-deprecating honesty. They don't shy away from talking about the pathetic aspects of being human, struggling with them, and at the same time being a part of them. They are honest. And any person who talks honestly about themselves becomes human in your eyes—even though they are famous. An example of this is Mike Tyson—I don't know why I keep going back to him.

You aren't shocked when you find out that they may have abused drugs in their past, or used to be self-destructive in many ways. You actually half expect them to have done those things and made many mistakes. There is an element of seeing them as people, unlike those perfect beings.

Such people mock and criticise these perfect aspirational beings from time to time, by pointing out the obvious strangeness in the way they live, in how they advertise themselves, and the image they portray. In these moments, you too are able to see the bullshit which is so far removed from the experiences of normal people. But this clarity goes away in a few moments. It happens because clarity appeals to your reasoning; perfection appeals to your emotions.

That is why even though you may theoretically say: *it's all bullshit*. On a deeper, emotional level, you desire and are affected by it nonetheless.

From this broad group of people, you take entertainment as well as intellectual value. You admire them, not follow.

THOSE DEFINITELY NOT WORTH GIVING A SHIT ABOUT

4. *Those with high impact and perfection.*

This is advertising at its finest. PR firms **create** public personas and manage public perception to basically **sell you** the idea of perfect people. It's a highly developed system, involving psychological models and studies, manipulation of information, the creation of personas, the running of campaigns, planting news stories, scripted interviews, preservation of a narrative, social media utilisation, analysing the responses of people to different behaviours, and changing perceptions when required.

Ever hear a famous person say in the middle of an interview: 'My publicist is not gonna like me for saying this'…? Well, that's because that publicist is considering all of the above.

These narratives are in place and you have been trained to react to them without thinking. So what happens now is, anybody can pick up a narrative, and as long as they follow the instructions, you remain convinced that they are perfect. This is how this shit works, if you wanna get a following. And depending on whichever desire is dominant in you with respect to your age and maturity, you make your choices.

For example, if you are a teenager or guy in your early twenties, single, virgin, the narrative which might appeal to you would be: a guy with a great body and millions in his bank account, owns fast cars and big houses, has sex with beautiful models, and is always surrounded by gorgeous girls.

There is no honesty, only **advertisement** at all times to their target audience.

They don't have to say they are perfect beings: it's a by-product of the narrative. All they have to do is manage to be at the **centre** of everything you fantasise about and desire.

For many young women, the narrative sold is a perfect beauty which encompasses luxury, elegance and a lifestyle that does not make sense. But it has to not make sense, or else it wouldn't be perfect in your eyes. With a flash of common sense, you could look at it and conclude that it's a narrative that cannot be translated into day-to-day reality. But you only focus on aspects that deal with desire, fantasies and aspirations. You look to compare and feel bad.

And this shit doesn't stop here. The narratives go in all directions: the perfect happiness, the perfect success, the perfect wealth, the perfect intelligence, the perfect morality, the perfect leader, and on and on. Whatever it is, there are people selling perfection in that desire, to that market.

No wonder you hardly ever look within; you are too busy looking outside for answers as to how you can be like them.

The majority of this occurs on the internet, which makes social media platforms a cesspool of these narratives. This means the more time you spend on them, the more dishonesty you are exposed to. Basically, the more time you spend on these platforms, the more likely you are to dislike yourself; you will tend to see yourself as unsuccessful; be more and more unappreciative of what you have and the people you have in your life; become more desirous of material things; wish to be someone you are not; try to behave in ways that don't come naturally to you; and want to look like someone else. All because some run-of-the-mill person has the tools to manipulate data, eliminate aspects of being human and appear perfect to you.

This can be found in many people on YouTube, Instagram, Facebook, Twitter and whatever social media apps there are and are yet to come.

Then comes their upgrade, which is politicians, movie stars, musicians, writers, motivational speakers, journalists, activists, models, millionaires, billionaires who are backed by an array of people—counsellors, agents, publicists, managers, script writers, public relations firms, marketing teams, all working very hard to assure they remain fictional beings to you.

HOW TO SAVE YOURSELF FROM THIS BULLSHIT

Your choices lie between your 'self' and perfect people. You may find it laughable that 'perfect people' is even an option. That's because you're thinking logically right now.

Search your feelings: how many people hold an unquestionable place in your mind? Do you think they are the best? Not the best at what they do, just *the best. He/she is the best.* If you have ever said that about anybody, they are perfect beings to you. They could be activists, journalists, late-night show hosts, ex-presidents, current presidents, spouses of presidents, prime ministers, motivational speakers, public intellectuals, celebrities, or billionaire philanthropists.

In your mind, these are either perfectly moral people or have perfect intelligence. They have written good books, say the right things, and care about the world. They exude likeability, and have not an inch of human aspect which you sense with people around you.

They are always positive when interviewed, consistently profound and humble. It is almost as if the interviews were scripted. Or maybe they are just clever people who know what to say at the right time. They seem as if they are more evolved.

After watching them, we feel as if we have been left behind and ought to catch up with them, and the only way to do that is by following them.

Here's what you do whenever you feel like doing that: Admire, never follow. Nobody can discredit their acts of charity and positivity, but you have no idea who they are as a person—none—except what is in their control and power to sell.

Let's really compare the choices: perfect people or self—which is the better authority to lead you?

THE SITUATION WITH THESE 'PERFECT' PEOPLE

The situation with perfect people is:

- They are possibly the most famous people in the world, and almost everybody around you loves and follows them too.
- They exist on all social media platforms.
- They dominate in terms of number of followers.
- After seeing their large following, you find their narrative trustworthy. After all, *millions of people follow them, millions of people aren't idiots, I too am not an idiot, so I will follow them too.*
- When you come across people who try to expose these narratives and urge you to see these people as people, you tackle it brilliantly by comparing the number of followers of the two. After all, popularity, money and fame are the best metric to determine rational thinking, right? All the most influential

philosophers, thinkers and writers were multi-millionaires and looked like models, everybody knows this. Yes, that is sarcasm.

- They sell perfection, basically dreams.
- You look up to them, and believe what makes them happy will make you happy.
- You rely on them for the solutions to problems that have been created because of the perfect narratives they sell. *I am not like them, I can't think like them, I don't look like them, I don't have what they have.*
- From whatever they provide, whether it is entertainment or information, deep down you know you watch them because of the aspiration element.

THE SITUATION WITH YOUR 'SELF'

The situation with your **self** is:

- It exists within you, not on social media.
- It is alone and underdeveloped and will take time and work to develop.
- If you developed and empowered your self, it will look out for you by providing the answers to your fantasies, desires and confused wants.
- It will also render comparisons pointless, as you won't be chasing after ideas that make others happy. You would be focused on making yourself satisfied,

which is a highly introspective process and stays personal.

- After making the self your authority, the need to follow anybody will cease to exist completely.

The aspirational aspect means going in the opposite direction from your 'self'. No wonder it requires persuasion with advertising. The rest is taken care of by the narratives already created in this world—which make you assume that these people are fucking superheroes. Just chill with the assumptions, mate. This whole game is just their advertising and our stupid assumptions.

CHAPTER FIFTEEN

DON'T SUCK-UP IN A RELATIONSHIP

WHEN YOU MAKE LOVE YOUR AUTHORITY

Now we're gonna talk about the most common way in which people give their authority to another person: in love.

For a lot of people, love is the idea that someone else will make you happier than your self can. Right off the bat, that is a terrible idea. If both the parties believe that, it will lead to co-dependence, and if only one of the two does, it will lead to one becoming the other's servant.

When you are convinced that being with this person will make you happier, you suspend altogether the need for self-respect—that was your happiness index, but now this person is what brings you happiness.

You have to understand where your self-respect comes from. Self-control has to kick the shit out of any tendency in you that will stop you from living peacefully and performing at a gold-medallist level. That produces self-respect in you.

Now suddenly you have met a person you think is the only source you need to be happy. So, you start undermining your work, ignoring your other priorities, and make them the top one. It's understandable if it was like that only in the beginning—you both were excited then. But, if it has been years and you can't say no to them anymore; you fear that if you disappointed them, they will leave you; the only way to keep them is by doing whatever they wish to, then you've royally fucked yourself. They are your authority, and not in a cute way. This, my friend, is a successful invasion of your nation. Your nation now works for them—if you don't get what I am talking about, read Chapter 10: You Are A Nation.

WHY YOU ARE TRAPPED IN A GARBAGE RELATIONSHIP

There are many reasons why people get trapped in shitty relationships. Let's talk about them:

- *You think that you will never find a person as good looking as them; you will never find a person as great at sex as they are.*

- *You will never be able to love somebody again; nobody understands you better than them.*

If you are stuck in a shitty relationship and these are your reasons, then you need to hear some truths. First, these are highly over-exaggerated assumptions; two, stop trying to predict the future. Unless you are seventy years old and have had all sorts of experiences, you need to shut the fuck up.

Every person in a relationship thinks their partner is special. Wow! According to that logic, every single person in a relationship is special. If so many people in this world were special, the word 'special' would have no meaning.

They are not special; you are making them that because you have had limited experiences in life. It's a fucking assumption you are making. There are billions of people. He/she is not the only one. But the person you most definitely need to find first is your 'self'. Only then can you start to make sense of this.

Here are more reasons:

■ *You will never find a person who would love you again; you think you are not worthy; therefore, you are lucky to have them.*

This is a person who has convinced themselves that they are less. This insecurity might be one of the reasons you fear they will leave you for someone 'more deserving'. At the same time, it may also be why you love them— because you believe nobody else will want you. You do understand this is fear talking. But you have shared an apartment with this fear for such a long time that you genuinely believe that. Now, because of this fear, you have built a tolerance for their shit. In any case, the answer cannot be only this person. You have no data to support that, only your dumb fear is telling you that. This is a hugely bad assessment.

■ *You have put so many years and so much effort into this, so you can't back out or else you would look like an idiot.*

So your self-image is more important than peacefulness in your life? Great, then. If anything, it should be an even bigger reason to get out. You have spent a huge part of your life taking this shit; at least the remainder of it should be lived on your terms.

■ *You say that you are prepared to end this any second, you don't give a fuck anymore; but it keeps going on.*

This is a person holding on to a hope called: 'they will change'. You are watching the same movie every day, hoping that the ending will change this time. You secretly hope that they will change and reform with your tolerance and dedicated love. What happens is, once in a while, they are nice to you. You translate these actions as **indications** that they care about you, and tell yourself, *this is **who** they really are.* This, of course, is bullshit. When the bad experience returns, you aren't shocked, because it's the same movie all over again. The truth is, you aren't prepared to end this. What you have prepared yourself to do is keep taking shit from them. And once you have normalised it, why would you want to escape from it? It's a routine to you now.

■ *You believe they are who you **think** they are.*

This one just takes the cake. So, hear this out: the idea is that you are the only person who **truly** knows them. Again, you believe you know them like nobody else does. You created this idea because you have had intimate moments with them in which you saw them in their emotional highs and lows.

Well, this of course is an assumption—that you are the only person who has seen them in these emotional states. But you want to believe that, because you get a sense of personal connection with them, as if you were their family. And they probably say this shit to you too, which enforces this idea.

And because of this, you cannot leave them despite how horrid their behaviour may become because, in your mind, that would be like abandoning your family. You think that they don't have anybody like you in their lives. You are their protector, caregiver, mother, and they are supposedly orphans or damsels in distress.

■ *They need you because you're the only one who knows what's good for them. Therefore, they are harming themselves by pushing you away.*

This is taking the last idea and climbing the mountain of crazy. This is farthest from the truth and your bullshit justification. Here's what you need to hear:

If they left you, then they didn't need you in the first place. If they didn't leave you, but didn't do much to keep you either, then they were in the relationship for selfish reasons only. If they didn't leave, but have lied to you, cheated on you, then they never valued you like you thought they did. By no stretch of imagination are you the only person who truly knows them and is like their family. If you were, they would have shown you that in actions, not words.

Are you trying to fix somebody's life?

■ *They only have me. He/she is a broken person, and I am fixing them.*

Is *your* life completely fixed? Are they in their twenties or above? Can they read? Do they have internet? If **yes**, then they can fix themselves if they want to. Nobody can fix someone who doesn't want to fix himself/herself. Why don't you fix your own fucking life? There is plenty of help out there—books, videos, therapy, sensible people—if they need it. Stop pitying people. You have a fantasy that if you fix someone, they will love you back. So you look for broken people. Well, here's the truth: they are not the only ones. Everybody is. Everybody above the age of twenty-five is carrying some serious scars, including you. Mind your own fucking business. And here's news for you: they are not weak either. That's why they are fucking you up in a relationship. You're the one getting hurt.

Trust me when I say this, the logic that 'if you fix somebody, then they will love you' doesn't work—people don't work that way. They have their own minds. People are gonna do what they wanna do. If you want to know who somebody is, focus on what they do every day, what actually fascinates them, and how they behave around people. That will show you in which direction they want to go. The sooner you gather the strength to accept the truth, the better it will be for your future. Stop with this selfish charity. If you have so much time and energy, put it in your life and find a stable person who wants stability in relationship too.

HOW TO SET YOURSELF FREE FROM A BAD RELATIONSHIP

Step one: Decide once and for all that you want to leave.

Step two: You have to **see** them as oppressors, even if they are highly respected, loved, one of the nicest people in the eyes of others. It is absolutely necessary for **you** to see them as oppressors, if you want to break free.

Step three: Seek help from capable, caring people.

Step four: Be completely invested in **knowing** your 'self', because it will provide you all sorts of amazing possibilities for your future.

Step five: The most important step—once you leave, never ever look back. Do not try and find out what is happening with them, how they are, what they are doing, what they are uploading on social media. Close that chapter completely from your life.

HOW TO NEVER GET TRAPPED IN A SHITTY RELATIONSHIP

You need to have your concepts clear about what a stable relationship is supposed to be:

- A relationship does not mean giving a person authority over your self.

- In a relationship, self-respect should never be compromised or replaced by anything. The happiness from companionship comes from the need to be loved, understood and valued by someone. Self-respect comes from self-control. There is no correlation.

- Self-control will ensure continued respect from your partner. Knowing who you are and staying true to yourself will give you credibility and trustworthiness in their eyes.

- A relationship should be looked at as a partnership between the two people. Therefore, careful selection of a partner is required, not a random choice out of desires, urges and tendencies, which are the criminal elements.

- Finally, the self must always remain supreme. That doesn't mean you won't become habituated to the other person, or even addicted to them. The supremacy of **self** helps maintain the thin line between addiction and dependency. If the relationship doesn't work out, the addiction will wear off gradually after months, but dependency is a virus which makes you think there is no option but the other person. So, despite knowing that this relationship is toxic, mentally abusive or breaking all the unacceptable rules, you are unable to break away. You think that, without them, you don't exist—that is the poison of dependency. What you need to know and feel in your life is, you have your 'self' at all times.

From this, you can imagine why working on your 'self' is so important. Others don't dare to fuck with your nation if you have a strong leader. And when they do, the leader knows how to take care of you. Your 'self' is what you have—why not get busy knowing it and empowering it!

CHAPTER SIXTEEN

LEARNING HOW TO THINK

Ah, you have made it to the penultimate chapter: welcome and congratulations, mate. This might possibly be the most important chapter, and really heavy too. So, 'let's just jump into it'.

'How to think' is basically not knowing what to think. There you go. It's as simple as that. Well, not really; I mean, if you understood it, then it really is that simple.

The problem is that it's a simple idea that has been made too complicated. So, to reach that simple part, we will have to first get rid of the complicated bullshit.

First, I must acknowledge something. 'How to think' may be a confusing phrase to you. You might call it critical thinking, logical thinking or higher thinking of some sort. How I see it is in a simple way: a person who knows 'how to think' properly.

So, let's begin. I am sure you have heard of phrases like: think differently, out-of-the-box thinking, open your mind, rewire your brain.

They genuinely sound like amazing abilities, but the problem is, you don't know how to do that. They seem like impossible, unique things to achieve, and it becomes a fantasy in your mind. You may think it means thinking like Sherlock Holmes, or some wise, religious figure, or some bearded guy with forty degrees to their name. So, the way we start seeing it is like this: people who know 'how to think' are equipped with a superior intelligence, knowledge and understanding of how this world works. Their mind works better than yours, they know more than you, and they think better thoughts than you.

Then you wonder, *how do I learn to think the way they do?* It becomes a superpower in your mind, and such people become evolved beings. Achieving it, becomes a fantasy.

THE FANTASY OF HAVING HIGHER INTELLIGENCE

When something that cool-sounding becomes a fantasy, it becomes a highly sought-after thing by a lot of people. So, it largely takes people to three places:

1. *People join cults in the name of higher thinking.*

Since it is a type of intelligence that seems impossible for normal mortals to achieve by themselves, the process of developing this ability becomes a Hollywood movie in your mind.

You think it involves higher learning; sitting on the same spot, eyes closed for hours on end, thinking about nothing; learning mantras in a language you don't understand, repeating them, and translating them on Google. Upon reading the translations, finding out there is no sudden change in your thinking, feeling a hint of disappointment as it didn't even make you think, you thereafter convince yourself they are too profound for your current state of limited understanding. A lot of people are doing this. Good for them.

2. *People think they will become fictional characters.*

Since it is a fantasy, in your mind, achieving it will bring you acceptance and popularity, because you'd practically be like a genius fictional character.

The truth is, it doesn't change how the world treats you, because the world remains the same. However, you will learn how to deal with shit in a better way.

3. *People become followers.*

Because it's a fantasy, you become a follower of people who claim to have this ability. You start relying on them for solutions to your problems, become dependent on their programs, classes, workshops, and are willing to spend any amount of money because you believe that you will attain what they have at the end. That doesn't happen either, because if you did, then how will they earn?

Anybody can learn how to think. It's rather dull, and requires from you a lot of commitment over a span of years. You might think: *Years? Fuck that!* That's understandable, but it doesn't mean you can't focus on other things. Pursue whatever you want. This ability is built silently and simultaneously in the corners of your mind.

THE WAY YOU THINK RIGHT NOW

The way you think right now depends entirely on how you were taught to think as a kid. You are most curious at that age. So, at that age, whenever you were curious about something, there is a huge possibility that you were given a packet of information about that thing. And that was meant to make you satisfied and stop thinking about it. This is what it is, kid, move the fuck on.

When this became your method of thinking, packets of information came from three sources:

- From parents, friends and people that you trusted.
- From television shows, movies and people you watch on the internet.
- From your own feelings, based on your personal experiences.

You didn't learn to doubt, question, or how to formulate your own opinion. Your method became relying on packets of information, and believing them.

And when you believe them, you receive a sense of satisfaction which closes the need to further think about it. You think you know about it now. The thing is, it has remained unchanged to this day. That's how you still think.

Let's take an example. Somebody asks you: *How do I get a girlfriend?* In your mind, you will look into all the information you have on what girls like, what girls want, and what a guy should do.

These packets of information make you believe that you know the answer to his question, even though this knowledge has hardly ever been experimented or questioned, compared to other alternatives and theories. There is no information on the longevity of the results.

You actually haven't even considered these things. The curiosity of finding out has been replaced by the satisfaction from knowing—even if it is bullshit. But because you have been trained to look for information from the outside, if one packet doesn't work, you look for another, since countless others are available just a click away.

This is also why most of your problems remain unsolved. You rely on packets of information instead of **thinking** about it yourself. You seek some magical information that will solve your problem immediately, somebody who will guide you and explain to you what you need to do.

ARE YOU ABLE TO SOLVE YOUR PROBLEMS?

Do you start searching for articles and videos the moment you have a problem? Before reading the articles with the hope of a detailed magical solution, do you first sit down and try to solve the problem, going point by point, by **thinking** on your own? You don't. You're habituated to receiving solutions, ideas and information from others. So, how do you expect to learn how to think when you hardly ever practise thinking!

Whenever somebody comes to you with a problem, you do the same with them as well. You give them packets of information the same way you give it to yourself from the internet or other people. That does three things:

- The focus is never entirely on solving their problem.
- The focus is more on the duty of providing help and how that makes you feel. *I feel so happy that I helped them.*
- The focus is on selling that you know what you are talking about, because you don't want to appear incompetent, which really is a sign of incompetence.

THE TRUTH ABOUT INTELLIGENCE

So, thinking differently, in theory, requires two simple things:

- Discovering a new way of looking at something; a way that you haven't thought of until now.

■ Since it is a new way of looking at something, you would have to ignore what you would normally think of that thing.

For example, we live in a time where the majority of news media organisations tell us what to think, what to feel and what to say. They don't leave any space for a person to make up their own mind about it. This is teaching humans 'what to think'. This training begins at a very early age, and unfortunately, in many cases, the first people to do this to children are their parents.

'How to think' is the opposite of that. It's a way of thinking in which you use your mental faculties and make up your mind independent from any influence, narratives and bullshit being sold to you.

This is an oversimplified example to give you a sense of what I am talking about.

So, the first step of developing 'how to think' requires you to not know how to see the thing at first. It requires you to be clueless; because only then you will start to look for clues.

And for you to start looking for clues, you will have to abandon all the ways you learned how to see things from before. Only then can you come up with a new way of seeing it. This is how creative thinking works as well.

I will tell you once more in a different way. When you have to think about something, you forget every single thought that existed before about it. You start from zero. You start from: I don't know.

I understand if even now it feels a bit heavy. There is a reason for it. We live in a world that largely celebrates knowledge, not intelligence. And when having knowledge is enough, most people don't care about thinking. Actually, most people think that knowledge is intelligence, and they cannot be more wrong.

The idea that a person who has several degrees is intelligent is a highly misplaced idea; but we think like that. So, in school, we teach kids to learn as much as they can. Learning can be achieved by hard work. What about teaching kids how to think? We don't do that yet.

A degree is a certificate of skills; therefore, someone with degrees is a person skilled in those subjects, not a fucking thinker. And without the ability to think critically and creatively, people largely remain unimaginative skilled workers.

This has insane implications in all areas of our lives and the way we think as a society, because this is exactly how we become followers as well. Let's dive into this properly.

WE LIVE IN A WORLD THAT CELEBRATES KNOWLEDGE, NOT INTELLIGENCE

We live in a world in which, if you have knowledge, then you are a cool person. People will think you are competent.

I am not saying it's a good thing or a bad thing; it's just how things are, okay?

When knowledge makes you cool and competent, then your focus shifts from thinking what that knowledge means, to collecting it. And when you are simply collecting information, it doesn't make you think very much, because that's not your objective.

Your objective is to be cool; after all, that impresses people—what else do you need! Take the example of a kid who decides to be at the top of their class; they are learning on an incredible level, but not really thinking about what they are learning, because that's not their objective. It is to top the class.

Therefore, in this world, the battle is over who knows more, or who can show they have more knowledge—that's what we are running after. Most people don't even know what the fuck intelligence actually means. No wonder reading is emphasised so much by people, but not thinking.

Knowledge is a great thing when the objective is to make you think. It is a superpower when you use it to make better decisions in your life. Knowledge is what enhances your intelligence, because it is food for your thought. But when you don't know how to use knowledge or data, and it is being used to show-off—that reveals a lack of intelligence.

THE PROBLEM WITH THE WAY OUR WORLD THINKS

When having knowledge becomes a sign of competence, not knowing becomes incompetence. So if you say: *I don't know*—that's incompetence. People might think you are an idiot, uninformed, ignorant ... you get the idea.

Now, if you remember, when we were talking about how to think differently, the first step requires you to be clueless; it requires you to say, *I don't know*. Only then can you begin to think about it in new ways.

When we live in a culture where that is punished, where immediately choosing sides, or always having a strong opinion is the norm, thinking gets punished. We discourage it without even realising it. Therefore, our opinions become either first reactions to information, or learning 'what to think' from other sources.

The truth is, it takes time to formulate a solid opinion on something. When you are thinking, it might even take days. But in a world where people claim to be experts on issues they have no idea about, it's really hard to stay clueless and think—even for a short while. No wonder we have left wing and right wing, and thousands of other groups in everything. No one wants to just wait and think about something from all perspectives.

Every person is sure they have figured the whole thing out, whether it is politics, modern technology or an environmental or social issue. When having knowledge is competence, anybody who disagrees with your stolen opinions becomes an idiot, and someone who has no opinions becomes straight-up confusing—*who the fuck even is that guy! Don't you care? Are you selfish? Please pretend it matters to you so I can share this clever opinion I've stolen from somebody and feel superior? Please debate me.*

The thing is, when only knowledge is valued, one can get it from anywhere, because the source doesn't matter. The source could be:

- An article. You scan through the information, and then borrow the author's opinions. You might also believe you have as much of an understanding of the issue as an expert.
- A friend, who has told you what they learned, which you then later recite as your own research.
- News comedy shows; not realising comedy is only meant to make you think, not tell you what to think.
- News sources, which are flag-bearers of selective ideologies.
- Reading only the headlines of articles and what people are saying in the comments section.
- What people you respect are saying. What the famous people you follow are saying. What the group you follow and identify with is saying.

All of the above teach you what to think. And this is how we appear competent in this world—none of which comes from 'how to think'.

WE DON'T KNOW SHIT

If you wanna be intelligent, my friend, you have to accept that you don't know shit. Whatever you have been taught until now came from somebody telling you what to feel and what to think.

We live in a world where we have already built **narratives.** These narratives create two sides or more. When having knowledge makes you competent, you obviously want to know about stuff and have opinions too. When we don't take the time to think and do research on our own, we let our feelings do our bidding. So whichever narrative makes sense to our feelings is the one we choose. After that, you rely on the people from the narrative you have chosen to tell you what to think. How do these narratives work?

One side uses information to create opinions that support their narrative, such as *immigrants are evil.* The other does the same, *immigrants are just like us.* With more and new information, the sides either lose or win. But they keep defending and attacking and the circus of narratives continues endlessly.

The reason why you might be sure that what you know is right is because the narratives have sold it to you pretty convincingly. It's just brilliant salesmanship. What you fail to realise is: you have to rely on them because you don't know what to think. You actually don't know shit.

Any person or any expert who claims that they know for sure doesn't know what they are saying. An expert in the same field from a hundred years in the future will tell them the limitations of what they know. In a true sense, we know only a little. And yet, not knowing stuff is considered as a sign of incompetence.

WE ARE INCOMPETENT AND COMPETENT AT THE SAME TIME

Let's quickly settle the debate about what makes us competent as well. We are humans. We are really competent in some things, and totally suck in a lot of other things. We are both competent and incompetent at the same time.

The problem is our dumb assumption that if somebody is competent in one field, they must be awesome in all other aspects. Unfortunately, that is how we form impressions. *'They are very competent at this thing; therefore they must be great overall.'* Nope. Having great skills, vast knowledge, and experience in a thing most definitely makes you competent in that thing **only**. For example, a person could be a competent programmer, but that doesn't make them a competent person overall. No way does it indicate that the same person is competent in aspects of thinking, behaving, perceiving and creating.

Similarly, how to think does not make you competent in all respects either. All it does is make you competent in thinking-related aspects; for example, you will become better at decision-making.

The whole idea of wanting to see people as either competent or incompetent is another dumb shit thing we need to get rid of. People are people—that's how you need see things.

WHY IS IT SO HARD TO THINK DIFFERENTLY

In plain terms, the two stages of thinking differently are:

- Not knowing or cluelessness
- Wanting to know

This would have remained this simple if we had not brought 'what to think' into our minds and lives. This is what the stages look like now:

- Not knowing
- Learning 'what to think'
- Abandoning 'what to think'
- Wanting to know

Abandoning 'what to think' is the hardest thing. Not just because you have been trained. No, sir, it's because you have become a follower of narratives and ideologies. You see the world a certain way, and abandoning what to think would require abandoning that too. I know; your feelings are involved; there is a sense of community; you are following so many groups and pages; you have made friends; you may even think it is your identity now. It can be hard.

Maybe if we talk about them, it will be easier.

HOW THEY MAKE YOU A FOLLOWER

You follow **narratives**. Narratives are basically templates on how to see things. Narratives use and twist historical data, present-day information, your feelings, ideal scenarios, your lack of data, and salesmanship to build themselves and spread. If you can see this pattern, you will be able to free yourself immediately.

For example, let's take the narrative that dinosaurs didn't exist.

- It twists historical data—basically **uses** what supports the argument, and denies and discredits what doesn't.
- It twists present-day information by creating theories that discredit the evidence.
- It uses your feelings, such as, in this case, scepticism and love of God.
- It uses an ideal scenario, which capitalises on your scepticism, like it's a conspiracy theory by the government, atheists, scientists or whoever to discredit religion and to propagate science over religion.

- It capitalises on your lack of data and laziness to research it on your own.
- Lastly, a convincing, charismatic figure is used as the spokesperson. A person that makes you think, *he looks like he knows what he is talking about.*

There are a host of narratives present in this world. We all follow a few. The most prominent ones would have to be: Our nation is the greatest. Our religion is the greatest. Our culture is the best. Our nation is going to be the greatest if we could get rid of a few people. This other nation is our enemy. This group of people is violent. Our culture is under threat. This group of people is inferior. Science is evil. And on and on.

They are not even complicated. Just remember the script:

- It uses and twists historical data selectively to suit the narrative.
- It uses and twists present-day information to create an aura of fear or anger.
- It uses your feelings.
- It uses an ideal scenario, either one from the past or in the future.
- It capitalises on your lack of data and facts.
- Lastly, convincing, charismatic voices and figures are used as spokespersons.

For example, take 'our nation is the greatest', put it through the script, and the narrative built is:

- Our nation used to be the greatest.
- The nation is not the greatest anymore.
- Don't you want the nation and people to rise again?
- We will rise and prosper if we did this or that, for example, elect this person.
- Here are all the people, political parties and nations we can blame for our current situation.
- Lastly, politicians, news anchors, celebrities, lawyers, social media personalities are used as spokespersons.

You are highly influenced by whichever narratives you follow. And it doesn't matter if it is right wing or left wing or whatever—they all use the same pattern. Facts and logical reasoning isn't left or right wing, nor do they give a shit about ideology. So, if you think you practice reasoning and common sense, you wouldn't give a fuck about ideology and narratives either. You'd find shit on both sides. The question is: do you?

YOUR PERSONAL EXPERIENCE IS NOT THE BEST TEACHER

You change the way you think from your personal experiences as well. A good experience might shape your entire perception of that thing or person in a positive light. Similarly, a bad experience can do the opposite. The truth is, they are not the greatest teachers. The perceptions you may create from personal experiences are very limited in data, highly dependent on your environment, and may exist only in **your** personal reality. That is incomplete and highly unreliable data.

For example, in the beginning of a relationship, when everything is going great, your perception of people in general might become, *people are great, life is so great.* But if you are left or cheated on by a person, your perception might become: *everybody is selfish. All men are assholes. All women are gold-diggers.*

Another example is, when people travel to a country they have never been to before, and because of a good experience, they form the perception, *people of this country are very nice. They are just great.* That is a generalisation based on your personal experience. Someone else's experience might be the opposite of yours.

Therefore, such learning tends to become easy to recruit by narratives and ideologies. For example, if you have had a bad personal experience with foreigners, you might join the narrative that 'foreigners are bad' and generalise. If you had good experiences, then you might join 'foreigners are great', and also generalise. Simple common sense will tell you: they are just people.

When it comes to your personal experiences, try to remind yourself that they have not taught you everything you need to know. The world doesn't revolve around you, so there's a huge possibility that your interpretations may be wrong; that maybe you don't know everything about it; or maybe you don't know anything about it at all. It's not a bad place to be—to not know about something. You can find out more about anything only when you admit to yourself that you don't know.

WHEN YOU ABANDON THE WAY YOU CURRENTLY THINK

Just to remind you, here's an example of how you may think right now:

When you are asked a question that requires your point of view, your mind immediately starts looking for all the packets of information that you may have on the topic. You might remember interviews you watched, in which a person gave an answer to the same question. You may remember a podcast that dealt with the same question. Once you recall these, you give your answer with great confidence.

These recorded answers and stolen perceptions—even though they may convince and impress others—prevent you from thinking and creating your own perceptions. As impressive as they may be, they are not yours. Also, because they are not yours, they largely remain unapplied in your day-to-day life.

'How to think' requires two things:

- Abandonment of **all** the packets of information or perceptions you may have collected so far.
- Getting to know or finding out by relying on **data** and **thinking**.

By rejecting all these packets of information, you are training yourself to think on your own. It is also accepting that a lot of your previously held views might have been one sided.

When you were a follower, you stopped seeing data as data; instead you got stuck with wondering, what narrative does this data serve? This made you purposely ignore information that challenged the narrative you followed.

You started viewing it as a war between my narrative—which is good—and the other—which is evil. You became so caught up with this idea that every time real data was presented to you that could have impacted your perceptions, the first thing you cared about was the source: which website is this from? Therefore, data became unimportant, facts become secondary; the source became everything. If the source was in the list of enemy narratives, the data became bullshit, even if it contained facts supported by evidence. *This is right-wing propaganda. That is liberal propaganda.* This made your perceptions one-sided, controlled and chosen by the narratives.

Once you free yourself from all narratives and the packets of information, and seek only data, you realise how much you had closed yourself to learning and developing your thinking.

DATA IS A MIND-FUCKER

If you can look at data objectively, it has the power to completely change, improve, or destroy all your previous perceptions and ways of thinking. Here's an example of how data fucks with your mind: If you heard a common problem about marriage, you may think you have a solution because you have heard of this before. But as you get more and more information, you would see the problem becoming more complex, very emotional and very human. With new data, you may realise your older solution doesn't apply anymore.

The point is: your perceptions can always be challenged by new data. Our thinking relies entirely on whatever we know at present, which means we don't know much about anything. New data can come in any day and change that, or confirm it.

Another example of this is: when you see a couple for the first time, you may form a perception of their relationship and who they are. Later, with more data, you may realise your previous perception was completely wrong.

YOU ALWAYS STAY AT NOTHING AS A THINKER

In a way, 'how to think' becomes a continuing, never-ending struggle to know with certainty. By never-ending, I don't mean that you won't be able to solve anything. Of course, you will develop many perceptions, theories and impressive patterns of solving things. What it means is, you will always remain in doubt; you will always remain a student, and data will be your teacher forever. Even if you have theories that work and explain something wonderfully, you would be fully prepared to toss them aside for a better one.

You will have accepted that you actually don't know for sure, for two reasons:

- There is always new data that could render your explanations inapplicable.
- Your explanations are the best that your mind could come up with at this moment.

This keeps you humble and hungry. This also sharpens your mind more as you try to surpass yourself by coming up with a better explanation. For this, you consume more data, fill your mind with knowledge, and build better theories from it. You are unlike those who think they know everything. You can obviously destroy them in a debate; but, in your mind, you put yourself at nothing, and therefore remain a learner.

HOW TO BUILD SOLUTIONS AND PERCEPTIONS

Once you have abandoned 'what to think', in the beginning, you will feel clueless. It's the same cluelessness that you felt as a kid when looking at an elaborate puzzle for the first time. You do not know a pattern with which to solve it immediately. But once you believe you can do it and take up the challenge, you end up solving it. Three things happen afterwards:

- The second time you solve the same puzzle, you might end up solving it in a different way from the first time. Your memory may have failed to capture all the steps in your first success, so you can't repeat them. But, after several repetitions, you would learn to solve the puzzle with some definite patterns. Similarly, as you apply your thinking to solve a problem or create your perception of something, you would, by repetitions, at some point discover a few patterns which would loyally serve your mental faculties in solving similar puzzles in an efficient manner.

- These patterns might not solve all puzzles.

- The more elaborate the problem, the more evolved the patterns are forced to become. The same applies to perceptions. With an issue that has more complexities, you might have to rethink the entire pattern.

Most of all, 'how to think' means allowing the data to make you think; *not* your preconceived notions dictating to you how to feel about data. You learn only when you are open to learning. To develop how to think, you would have to **focus** on the **contents** of the problem with absolute disregard for your personal judgements, biases and prejudices. Only then can a new pattern and a new understanding take birth.

How to think differently is an ability that has to be personally developed by you with your own thinking. You're going to come up with your own patterns. This doesn't mean they wouldn't have existed before; it would mean that the patterns you have come up with would serve you the most and the best.

And now we move on to the last chapter.

CHAPTER SEVENTEEN

A FEW SIMPLE THINGS TO NEVER FORGET

LEARN TO SPOT BULLSHIT FROM A MILE AWAY

There are people who can sense bullshit of any kind from a mile away—that should be your goal. This means, when you are watching news or being sold anything, you are able to separate data from the narrative. Not to forget, narratives too have data about how people collectively think and how to make people think something they weren't thinking before. By studying narratives without getting recruited, you are able to locate the exact spot where the salesperson uses or twists the data, makes an emotional appeal to the viewer, and guides them on how to feel about the information.

From now on, look at all narratives as sources that have nothing to do with you. You can learn from them, agree with their analysis if it matches yours, entertain yourself with their theatrics, but never assume that they speak for you. You alone speak for yourself.

SOLVE YOUR OWN FUCKING PROBLEMS

This does not mean you should solve all of your problems at once or only when it has become so big that you can't sleep anymore, it's giving you panic attacks, you can't focus on anything else in your life, and you have started to call yourself a fucking idiot a lot.

This means that you have to solve your problems because you have to develop the mindset of seeing any problem, any red flag, any concern as something that needs to be dealt with immediately, regardless of whether it is minor or major, in the present or with the potential to occur in the future. The mindset of problem-solving recognises that problems are meant to be solved, acknowledges that a problem is a sign of something not working out, and builds the habit of solving them at the first sight of their presence.

Problem-solving should be a habit, not the last resort. If you considered the number of problems in your life currently sharing the status of being unsolved and your general approach to dealing with them, you would realise how far you have strayed from the course of developing your mind. The more problems you solve, the more you would know about yourself—and that's why you need to solve every last one of them.

Here's another thing, there is a chance that a lot of your problems might be coming from a source called fascination. Most problems created from this source come from its chief productions called comparing, envying, aspiring and desiring. So a lot of you are busy finding solutions to problems that don't even exist. You are creating them because you haven't been humbled by practical reality. You still live in the fantasy world.

For example, a person in a fine relationship comparing it with relationships of other people; comparing your partner with other people or someone you follow online; and from that, finding flaws in your relationship and the partner. That is a person looking to create problems because reality is not a romantic-comedy movie to them.

How can this be solved? By thinking and asking yourself, *what is the source of my problem?* And when you find out that it's your stupid insatiable fascinations and desires, you get to ask yourself, *why am I so obsessed with this perfect life, with these fascinations and desires?*

It's a deep question. It will make you think and question the nature of fascinations; you will realistically ask if they are even practically achievable, or are they just an unending struggle that keeps updating itself no matter how close you come to it?

And that is why it is most important that you solve your problems, because only by this habit do you come to find and spot real problems, distinguish between real problems and problems that don't exist. In short, the more you engage in solving your problems, the easier it becomes to locate the exact source of why you might be creating problems that do not exist.

IT'S ALL RIGHT TO FEEL PAIN

There are no great secrets hiding behind the doors of happiness, except that everything is great and is supposed to be great for you to remain happy. That is called a 'safe' life, and also an uninformed scared life.

You find out a lot about life, yourself, and others when you don't mind stepping outside of feeling happy. You find out what your limitations are, what you can take, what you can come back from, and what you can become. None of that can be learned and actualised by wishing to be safe and happy all the time.

You need to accept that experiences that are going to be highly unpleasant, disturbing and painful are going to come into your life. There are people who don't expect these things to ever happen to them, so they feel like victims when it does. In their minds, they feel like they never deserved to go through this. They see such experiences as happiness being robbed from them. Therefore, their conclusions and concerns float around who to blame and what to blame. *How dare this happen to me?*

Meanwhile, a person who doesn't mind feeling other things understands they are not alone in experiencing such shit. People go through this every day. It's nothing new. So, the focus remains in solving it and learning from it as much as possible.

In short, you have to accept that you are human. You will go through it all. You will at some point be ripped off, betrayed, taken advantage of, lied to, cheated on, defeated, laughed at, and treated unfairly. And at some point, you will make someone else feel a lot of these things too—no matter how good a person you tell yourself you are. There are also going to be times in which you will feel absolutely shitty about yourself. You may think you are lonely, ugly, unwanted, a loser, and basically a piece of shit.

The truth is, they are just emotions. You can go through them if you simply allow their presence in your mind. You should know that it's okay. It's okay to feel those things. Don't plan your escape, let them hit you. They will make you think. They will make you aware of the sources of the pain—both inside and outside. Isn't that how we learned to distinguish between what's safe and otherwise as children? Why do you want to stop that education? You will become wiser by acknowledging your vulnerabilities, not by covering them up with distractions. Allow yourself to feel pain and acknowledge it with respect, not fear. That's all the ointment pain needs—acceptance—and from then on, it starts to subside.

Allow yourself to feel pain, not because you can't help it, but because it has earned that place. You made a decision that brought pain to you. Don't fight it. Look at the decision which opened that door. That pain could be a reminder of how much you opened yourself to somebody. Fear would advise you to close yourself, never to trust again—that is the lesson of fear. If you have been betrayed, your reasoning would simply make the process of gaining entry harder—that is the lesson of pain.

When you ask, *All right, what's the solution?* Your focus goes directly to the problem, not feelings. Therefore, your reasoning takes charge, not your crumbled state of emotions. And when your reasoning is in charge, you gradually discover several truths.

NEVER COMPARE YOURSELF TO ANYBODY

You are you. The more time you spend learning and trying out what makes others happy and what others do to seem impressive and cool, the more time you are wasting. Ultimately, all that is going to matter is knowledge of your self—that is the only thing which will make sense, and the only thing that will give you any satisfaction in life, regardless of your age, what your net worth is, and what your relationship status is. The knowledge of you is what matters. If you don't realise this now, time will eventually make sure you find out about it, but then it may become too late.

You are not them. If they are ahead of you, don't make them your enemy, nor become their follower simply because you may not want to go where they are going. Both competition and being a follower have the tendency to corrupt your original motivation to do that thing. The world does not know you, so it will sell you what it sells to everybody. You might not know yourself either, so you will assume it will make you happy. Therefore, never be too sure of what is being sold to you. They are usually things that are meant to shut your reasoning down and blindly make you chase after things. We have talked about it already: advertising, assumptions, fascinations, remember? They can't work on you if you know what you want and what you don't want. The same applies to comparisons. If you know what you want in life, then you wouldn't care about what others have.

Always remember: Assumptions exist where data doesn't. And the only data worth collecting is about the 'self', and in the direction of what the self wants. Lastly, if you have ever told yourself that whatever you have in your life is less, then, my friend, terming it as less is a perception that is born only after you compare yourself to someone who has more. If you hadn't compared yourself, then what you have are perfectly fine tools, the most important of which is the ability to learn. With these tools, you can develop yourself and earn whatever you want. You can have whatever you want because several others from much worse conditions than you have done it, and continue to do so.

In comparing yourself, you will find all the reasons to be miserable, all the excuses to not take action, and all the wrong reasons to want to take action. But in not comparing, you find and focus on what you have at hand and making it better. If somebody has more than you, good for them. You have you, so use your mind and the ability to learn together.

WHAT DOES SMART, CLEVER, INTELLIGENT, WISE AND STUPID REALLY MEAN

What really is the definition of stupid? People tend to call anybody stupid based on how they feel at the moment. Stupid can be one who knows nothing, knows less, makes mistakes, isn't very articulate, does something they ought not to, does something slowly, is obsessed with physical appearance, doesn't take life seriously, or one who fails to follow instructions. People call politicians they dislike and won't vote for, stupid. A politician not only convinces people that his opponents are too stupid to govern, but proves by getting elected that people are too stupid to vote. A machine can be stupid, an animal can be stupid, an experience can be stupid, basically anything can be stupid.

When it comes to words like smart, clever, intelligent, wise and stupid, almost nobody cares to adhere to the meanings in the dictionary. We use them based on our understanding and feelings at the moment. Therefore, the first four are very often used interchangeably. So, keeping with the tradition, let's define these words in a manner you might find easier to use.

1. *A smart person*

A smart person is one who is more able than others in doing something. It could be someone who has a natural talent at something, a person who does something better than others, a person who learns something more quickly than others. I am sure you have seen when somebody doesn't need much explaining and is able to catch on very quickly, they are called smart.

2. *A clever person*

A clever person is one who knows how to use that ability for self-benefit. Basically, a clever person is not only smart, but knows how to use, capitalise on, and create benefits for oneself that are beyond the traditional course of benefits those abilities are known to provide, and aim to create much bigger opportunities for themselves. This is why such moves are called 'clever' moves. And that is why successful businesspeople, politicians, powerbrokers and other such people are called clever. For example, this world is largely led by clever people, and therefore their strategies, ideas and plans continue to focus on self-benefit rather than the benefit of the world.

3. *An intelligent person*

An intelligent person is one who works on becoming self-aware. We call somebody intelligent when they have some perspectives on questions and problems we find much confusion with. Upon hearing them talk, we say, he is really intelligent, because to you, they are making sense, or at least making you think from points of view to which you can relate. You may also refer to them as smart because you are impressed by their ability to produce interesting arguments and unexpected ways of looking at information. You regard this as something you haven't learned to do yet, thereby making them better at it, and therefore, really smart.

4. A wise person

A wise person is one who becomes self-aware. A wise person can also be clever but out of self-awareness chooses to be restrictive and free at the same time, therefore, wise.

So, what is left is stupid. Who is that? Everybody is stupid and nobody is stupid. Stupidity has everything to do with what you believe at a certain time. For example, your ego can make you believe a thousand things about yourself, and if you acted based on those beliefs, you would be a fucking moron in the eyes of people who know better. Let's take a more specific example: a person who thinks he is intelligent because he has read a lot, watched a lot, and memorised a lot, but missed out on thinking a lot. They are gonna look fucking stupid in front of a person who has done a lot of thinking. The examples can go in all directions; you will assume you know something for sure, but the result will show otherwise, and you might feel stupid. Out of overconfidence in your abilities, you might make claims which would be proven otherwise, and others might call you stupid. You would trust someone because you believe them, and after they betray it, you would call yourself stupid for ever trusting them. The scenarios are way too many.

We are all stupid at certain points of time because we all go through these things, we all have believed in ideas that we later realised were nonsense, and therefore, nobody is stupid forever because of our capacity to learn. Even the greatest minds act stupidly at times, and it is accurate to call them stupid for that. So, if you believe that you are incompetent or stupid, then you need to know that's because of a very common belief too. This belief is called: there are smart people and then there are dumb people—a lot of us believe that.

It obviously comes from comparison. You look at a smart person, compare yourself with them, and conclude: *wow, I don't have as much knowledge as they have. Therefore, I am fucking stupid.* The belief is that smart or intelligent people cannot be stupid because they know a lot, they can think very fast, they can talk very fast, and they produce very interesting arguments. So they are placed so high on a pedestal that in comparison you are bound to think of yourself as a moron. We have already talked about perfect people.

If you watch a lecture on a subject by a professor and think, *I am stupid for not understanding anything*, then based on the available data, the difference between you and that person is they have learned something which you haven't. That's it. This can be solved by you learning what they know. The point isn't that you should—unless you want to. The point is, you do not become stupid for not knowing things because things can be learned. Some of them may take very long, require painful sacrifices and discipline, but it can be done. People do this all the time.

It's not wrong to be impressed by amazing achievements or qualities, but concluding from that, *I can never think like them* is the belief that is making you stupid. Not only can you learn just about anything, you can learn how to learn anything, and you can also learn how to unlearn things—that is the true potential in you. Instead of the dumb belief that divides people into two intellectual classes, you need to start living your life with this truth. Empowering and degrading yourself are two sides of the same coin. Both require energy and time. It depends entirely on what you believe. So, do you wanna limit yourself and believe you can never think like somebody or do you wanna elevate yourself and believe you can learn anything in this world?

Don't forget, having wrong beliefs is what makes you stupid; it's the right ones that set you free. The only difference is the wrong ones are easily available, and you have to fight for the right ones.